MORE THAN MEDALS

Lessons From an Olympian

Betsy Mitchell & Ann Worthington

More Than Medals: Lessons from an Olympian
Author: Betsy Mitchell
Author: Ann Worthington
Editor: Taylor Brien
Cover Design: Nicole Wurtele
Interior Layout: Michael Nicloy

ISBN: 979-8-9881891-7-6

PUBLISHED BY CG SPORTS PUBLISHING

AN IMPRINT OF
NICO 11 PUBLISHING & DESIGN
MUKWONAGO, WISCONSIN
MICHAEL NICLOY, PUBLISHER
www.nico11publishing.com

Quantity order requests can be emailed to:
mike@nico11publishing.com

Printed in The United States of America

To my parents, Jim and Diane, for your unconditional support and teaching me to kick, kick, kick!

FROM THE AUTHOR

I have known for quite some time that I wanted to share my thoughts on amateurism, the potential positive power of sports in adolescent development, and the role of parents and coaches as essential to that process. I have written my thoughts while sitting on planes, trains, and in hotel rooms all over the world; privately reflecting, appreciating, and basking in the experiences of the first quarter of my life. What I wanted to ensure is that I never let my first twenty-five years be the best ones. I have always wanted more; to contribute, to help others, to pass it on, to give it back. People ask me about my experiences all the time and I'm happy to share, but I could never make my story coherent or organized when writing. The words flow differently when I am speaking and engaging with people directly.

My co-author Ann Worthington has been a North Star in my life for nearly forty years. During the last several of those years, I have asked, nudged, and implored until she finally relented and did the heavy lifting of writing this manuscript. After hours and hours of weekly scheduled calls, she organized my thoughts and teased them out of my brain. I know we think alike, which made it easier, but she is the real reason this book is complete. Thank you, Ann, for your partnership on this project and even more importantly for our years of friendship.

Although I hope readers enjoy this book, my primary goal is to inspire others to think differently about amateur sports. By sharing my experiences, I want to help young athletes and their parents along their path. And for parents, coaches, volunteers, and officials who come together to form our youth sports culture, continue your work, but be mindful of its impact on our children. Sports can benefit everyone if we set aside ego and take satisfaction from serving, guiding, and striving, not from winning.

In my life, personal is professional, and professional is personal. I enjoy a perfectly flawed human existence, filled with outstanding moments that began with amateur sports and a supportive family. It has not been all rainbows, butterflies, and unicorns. I've faced plenty of mistakes, missteps, and challenges along the way. To those who supported me, thank you. To those whom my mistakes affected, I am sorry but also grateful for your grace as I learned and found my path. I have done my best to always make each day better. I still have a long way to go in life, and I believe the best lies ahead!

Betsy Mitchell

P.S. If you want to connect with me for a motivational speech, program consulting or book signing, please go to my website, www.betsymitchell.us for contact information.

TABLE OF CONTENTS

INTRODUCTION

Gold, silver, and bronze medals. I won quite a few of them during my swimming career, but I refused to let the hardware define me. As fantastic as it felt to win a race, winning was never my true focus; it wasn't why I swam. Performing my best was my primary goal. As an athlete, I felt joy, accomplishment, and satisfaction, even if I didn't win a medal. I loved swimming and would have trained and competed regardless of winning. Early on, I found the process more impactful in my life than the outcome, a prime example of how sports can be a positive influence in human development.

My swimming career spanned nineteen years, from 1972 to 1990, age six to 24. Competitive swimming was so long ago for me, I rarely think about practices or competitions these days, and I seldom get in the pool. My most vivid memories from my youth are of road trips and team events that fostered lifelong friendships, worldwide travel opportunities, and the trial and error of training. Swimming is based on repetition, and through repetition, I honed my talent with hard work. I am proud of my effort and my accomplishments. More importantly, the lessons I learned along the way carried me forward to a rewarding personal life and career as an athletic director.

Current estimates show that about half of the children in the United States, or roughly thirty million, take part in amateur sports. The general assumption in our culture is that sports are good for kids. They're fun! Besides being enjoyable, sports provide an incredible experimental and learning laboratory. Kids benefit when they master new skills, improve their physical fitness, and take calculated risks. Participating in sports can boost confidence and allow children to develop the building blocks for success. Plus, athletes learn a lot about themselves from playing, training, and working with a team. They grow through regular practice, goal-setting, and interaction with non-parental adults.

My experience competing in youth sports was overwhelmingly positive and truly amateur. As a swimmer, I was not involved in a sport that developed professional athletes. I also grew up in an era before the internet, cell phones, and social media became pervasive. Entertainment meant playing outside, working jigsaw puzzles with my mom, and watching televised football games with my dad. Kids lived and played more like *The Bad News Bears* and less like "keeping up with the Joneses." I loved the challenge of sports and was never driven by the lure of money, fame, or self-importance.

I grew up in Marietta, Ohio with my parents, Jim and Diane, and my older brother Peter. Although the name on my birth certificate says Faith Elizabeth Mitchell, everyone, including my parents, called me Betsy. My parents didn't believe it proper to just name me Betsy, so as an homage to my grandmothers, Faith and Elizabeth, I earned both of their names. I struggled with this during elementary school each year when the teacher took attendance on the first day of class. "Is Faith Mitchell here?" The teacher would raise her eyes from the attendance roll and scan the room for the student who accompanied that moniker. I would grit my teeth and reluctantly raise my hand into the air. When the teacher pointed towards me, I announced, "Betsy Mitchell is here." [1]

---

1 I officially changed my name from Faith Elizabeth Mitchell to Betsy Mitchell in 1993 before I got married. My fiancé felt strongly that I take his last name, Wilson, and I had agreed. But when I saw my name on the proposed marriage license, Faith Elizabeth Wison, I was startled. That person was a stranger to me. Throughout my life, I had always been Betsy; whether on team rosters, in newspaper articles, or on record boards. By changing my name, I felt it matched my persona and preserved a bit of my authentic self.

Marietta is a small town, and considered part of Appalachia, across the Ohio River from West Virginia. The humble people who live in this part of the country appreciate hospitality, self-sufficiency, and traditional family values. Neighbors help neighbors when they can, and often greet each other on the street or in town. I still smile when I picture my house on Third Street with a broad front porch, red brick chimney, and towering oak and maple trees in the yard. Marietta is quiet, rural, and a beautiful place to grow up. Unless you were a girl who wanted to play T-ball.

"Girls don't play T-ball." It was 1972, and I was six years old when I heard those words. My dad had taken my brother and his friends to sign up for the summer league, but I was excluded. I am certain I insisted on playing, tugging on my dad's trousers, or stomping my foot in the dirt. It wasn't fair because my brother and his friends got to play sports, and I wanted to play, too. But the woman at the registration table was adamant: "T-ball is for boys only."

I don't remember how my dad responded. He may have attempted to soothe or distract me, or he may have even offered to buy me an ice cream cone; he knew I was miserable. I had always tagged along with my brother and his friends and had too much energy to hang around the house. On the way home, we drove past the local Young Men's Christian Association (YMCA). The marquis out front read: "Summer Swim Team." My dad turned into the parking lot, and I reassured him I knew how to swim. That day, I became a member of the Marietta Marlins and was overjoyed because I got to join a team and play as well.

Of course, as a child, I didn't know I would fall in love with swimming and have it occupy thousands of hours of my life, but I consider myself lucky. It was almost as if the sport had found me. And I never thought swimming would take me anywhere, except to the other end of the pool, but I was wrong. As I reminisce on my experiences, I want to share the lessons I learned from training, competing, and being a member of a team.

Amateur sports hold an important place in our society, and when conducted appropriately, they can guide, teach, and positively influence children. The word amateur, originally from Latin, means "to love." An amateur is a person who engages in an activity for pleasure or love of their sport rather than for professional gain. Adults need to be reminded of this as we instruct our kids and shepherd them through childhood. Based on my experience, sports prepare kids for more important challenges in life. This book speaks to the value of sports, and is for parents, coaches, and athletes of all ages.

CHAPTER
1

FOCUS ON FUN

We play sports and call them games. These words suggest we take part in sports for enjoyment. As adults, if we experience joy or satisfaction in an activity, we continue playing. It's the same with children. If it's fun, they'll do it. Whether a child is chasing after a soccer ball or diving off of a diving board, coaches and parents must ensure the activity is fun. Laughter and encouragement are key, instead of yelling and anger. Parents and coaches need to focus on children developing their skills, not on a team's record of wins and losses. Games are for recreation and amusement, and kids must like the activity, or they won't want to take part. And as children become teenagers, they must find added value in the endeavor, or they may turn their focus elsewhere.

My first memories of swimming were at the Marietta, Ohio YMCA. In the pool, I felt spry and buoyant, and I found happiness splashing around with other kids. I attended practice frequently and loved every minute in the water. Our team learned the four swimming strokes: freestyle (or crawl stroke), butterfly, backstroke, and breaststroke. The first three strokes came naturally to me, but

I always struggled with breaststroke. Even as I imagined a frog kicking its legs, I couldn't bend my knees the correct way and found it difficult to generate power from my kick. As a member of the YMCA, I made new friends and looked forward to the next practice so I could "play" in the water. Certainly, not all children find swimming practice fun. Swimmers spend hours face down in the water, staring at the black line at the bottom of the pool. The repetition of back and forth and back and forth, with little time for social interaction, isn't for everyone. But my Marietta YMCA coach, Jim Everett, made practice feel like play time.

There were only a handful of swimming pools in Marietta, Ohio, and most were outdoors, so they closed during the winter. The YMCA had a six-lane 25-yard indoor pool where most residents learned to swim. Every time I walked into that YMCA, it reminded me of a beehive. Parents and children buzzed around the gymnasium and the pool, attending classes and enjoying recreational sports. It also felt like family because the receptionist welcomed me by name before I entered the locker room to change into my swimsuit. I looked forward to being there, feeling independent and excited as I prepared myself for practice.

Coach Jim greeted us on the pool deck and cracked a few jokes to get us laughing and establish an atmosphere of fun on the team. He was one of my favorite coaches because he always had a smile on his face. After leading us in light stretching, we jumped into the pool and the real fun began. I relished racing against the older kids, swimming in relays during practice, and playing the game "sharks and minnows" on Fridays. We sometimes goofed off during training by standing on the bottom of the pool or pulling on a lane line. When Jim caught us, he would bark at us, but always with a smile. If everyone in the group worked hard and behaved during practice, we would play a game or dive for pennies as a reward.

Swim meets were fun, too. The atmosphere was upbeat and casual, like kids hanging out on the playground. Our team sat together in a corner of the pool deck or in a nearby gymnasium. Sometimes we sneaked under the bleachers to make towel tents and play cards. We also ate string cheese and powdered strawberry Jello with our fingers. At those meets, I wanted to do my best and swim fast, but I didn't think about winning or setting records; more importantly, I raced against myself to lower my own best times. My favorite events were sprints: 25s, and 50s; just one or two lengths of freestyle or butterfly in a 25-yard pool. And I always looked forward to the relay events when four swimmers competed in the same race. Like ducklings, we approached the starting blocks holding the same towel so we wouldn't get lost. I often swam my best times while on relays and loved standing on the deck at the end of the pool, cheering for my teammates.

Growing up in Marietta, Ohio, in the 1970s, I imagine my life was like that of many other children. I lived with my family, attended public school, and went to church on Sundays. My family had a terrier mutt named Shorty. We celebrated the holidays with my grandparents. I did chores around the house, like making my bed and setting the dinner table. During the summer, I attended camp. My favorite pastimes were playing cards and bothering my brother. I also joined a Brownie troop, took ballet, and learned to play tennis.

As the years passed, I spent less time in Girl Scouts, ballet class, and on the tennis court because to me, those activities weren't nearly as fun as swimming. The joy I felt diving into the pool was unsurpassed. In the water, I was a mermaid, a dolphin, or an underwater superhero. The challenge of swimming longer distances and becoming faster was a huge confidence boost.

I grew up in an active family. My dad ran track in high school and was an Ohio high school state champion in the 440-yard intermediate hurdles. He also briefly played basketball at Ohio State University. Calling it her "sport," my mom was an avid gardener, and did her best to turn our yard into an English garden. She created tranquil hardscape spaces surrounded by sculpted boxwood and colorful perennials. My brother enjoyed activities like basketball and baseball, and later captained his Marietta High School swimming team. We belonged to a country club that offered seasonal swimming, golf, and tennis. It was there that my mom taught me how to swim. Our family also spent summer vacations at a cottage on Lake Erie. Although I played other sports and dabbled in many activities, swimming captured my heart. I remember loving every second of every YMCA practice and every swim meet.

During my formative years as a member of the Marietta YMCA Marlins, I swam after school and competed in occasional meets on the weekends. If my family had other plans, I skipped swimming so the four of us could spend time together. Our family did not revolve around my brother's or my activities. My dad worked long hours as the president of a local bank and during the twenty years when he helped raise my brother and me, he quit playing golf, his favorite game. My mom was a teacher and school counselor. She later served as president of the local school board, coordinating her schedule with Peter's and my schedules. Despite leading busy lives, my parents did their best to prioritize family time.

On Saturdays, if there was a swim meet, I went with either my mom or dad, while the other parent stayed home with Peter or took him to a different sporting event. At swim meets, I felt energized by the activity on the pool deck. Coaches whistled, shouted, and cheered for their swimmers, and my body buzzed with excitement about racing and lowering my times. My parents, like other "swimming parents," volunteered to time the races or work the concession stand at weekend meets. They were unaware of the events I swam and couldn't recite my best times. They were happy for me when I enthusiastically told them about my races. If I mentioned I didn't swim well, they said something neutral yet encouraging, such as, "You'll do better next time." They never told me to work harder or practice more. They certainly didn't question the coach, argue with an official, or attempt to correct the mechanics of my butterfly stroke. Their usual question after a swim meet was, "Where should we eat?"

My parents knew how to swim, but they weren't swimmers. Their naïve unfamiliarity with the sport made them uninterested in the sets I swam during a workout and unconcerned about my overall training regimen. They didn't question me about the next swim meet or my goals for the season. Compared to most parents today, mine had very little interest in swimming, but my parents played an incredibly crucial role in my success. During those early years, they took care of the basics: driving me to practice, laundering my dirty towels, and preparing meals and snacks. Their unconditional support allowed me to be a kid and focus on fun.

During the past two decades, our society has expanded the concept of amateur sports and corrupted it with money, even turning youth events into commercial endeavors. It has become commonplace for parents to argue with referees and interfere with coaches. If you open a newspaper or sports blog, you'll likely read about the latest parent who embarrassed themselves by taunting the competition or punching an official. If we truly want children to benefit from sports, it's imperative that we turn back the clock and focus on fun. Fun means something different to each individual, and every child must find their own version of it. For some, it's joining a team that runs up and down a field playing flag football. For others, it's tumbling on a mat or jumping on a trampoline. Other kids prefer spontaneous, unorganized fun like rolling around the driveway on a skateboard or kicking a ball in the park.

Childhood is a wonderful time to test the waters and try different sports or activities. It's an opportune time to broaden a child's life and discover fun. It could mean being a member of a volleyball or baseball team or arranging a pickup game with friends after school. Perhaps fun means joining a ballet class or learning gymnastics or diving skills. For others, it may mean whizzing around on skates or skis, feeling the adrenaline of speed. Each person needs to explore their interests and find their passion, which could also be music, drama, art, or dance. Passion satisfies all people and validates human efforts to belong and feel worthwhile. Whatever your age, it's important to find your fun.

Between the age of six and 22, I swam consistently on teams with a coach, teammates, and a regular practice schedule. I had found my version of fun. During those years, I don't remember many times that weren't fun, but once, when I was in ninth grade, which was part of junior high school in Marietta, I had returned home after school, fretting and crying. I was 13 and my "boyfriend" had asked me to the school dance. I really wanted to go, but Friday swimming practice would make me late for the party. I wouldn't have time to get dressed and dry my hair. I felt conflicted about how to tell John. Would he understand or think that was stupid? Like most 13-year-olds, I wanted to be "normal" and spend more time with my friends. I also didn't want to disappoint my coach and skip practice.

When my dad walked into the house that day, it startled him to find me red-faced and sobbing in the hallway. I told him I wanted to quit swimming because it kept me from going to football games and school dances. My dad paused for a moment and stared at me with a perplexed look on his face. He is a man of few words, so when he spoke, I always paid attention. He told me I could quit swimming if that's what I wanted to do, but I could also continue swimming and go to the dance. I simply needed to tell my coach I would miss practice on Friday. As a young teen, I hadn't believed I could do both and quit swimming, anyway. It was what I thought I had wanted. But after one week of hanging out after school, watching television, and doing a lot of nothing, I realized I wasn't missing out; I was missing swimming. There was no such thing as "normal," only what felt right to me. I belonged in the pool and immediately returned to practice; the place I felt most comfortable, accepted, and happy.

The other times during my life when swimming wasn't fun came much later, during my college years. The lessons I learned during my childhood carried me through those uncertain times.

I am extremely lucky to have discovered swimming, an activity that captured my attention, focus, and passion at a young age. My mom insists I was incredibly stubborn as a child, with an independent streak. When I attempted a task like tying my shoes or learning to ride a bicycle, I insisted I could do it myself. My mom also claims my persistence and self-reliance were clear from a young age since I skipped kindergarten and began first grade as a five-year-old. Swimming suited me because it's an individual sport. I could exercise my independence and embrace the challenge of workouts, thriving on the repetition of practice sets. Training implies work, and I worked hard, but it was fun, not laborious. Practice always provided an opportunity to race swimmers in the next lanes, and I looked forward to swim meets and competitions to test myself. How long could I hold my breath? How fast could I kick my legs? The sport didn't feel like work; there was no stress or anxiety. To me, it was all about the prospect of racing and lowering my times – the ultimate fun.

Remarkably, I found every aspect of swimming enjoyable; at least that's how I remember it. The good far outweighed the bad, and the memories still make me smile. To this day, a scheduled and structured life makes me feel productive, as it did in my youth. It is unrealistic to expect every child to enjoy swimming as much as I did, but finding an activity or program that captivates a child is critical. Finding joy in a sport, activity, or on a team makes for a productive, happy, sustainable life.

This became clear to me as an adult when my years of swimming and competing were behind me. In 1991, I began coaching the women's swimming team at Dartmouth College in Hanover, New Hampshire. One day during the spring, a friend suggested I try rowing. "You would be good at it," she said. She was right!

Rowing requires long, powerful strokes that begin with bent legs and a strong core. After learning the basics of rowing a single scull, a boat where the oarsman pulls on two oars, I transitioned to a double or two-person scull. (There is also another event called sweep rowing where a pair, four, or eight rowers each hold a single oar.) Rowing a double scull is difficult because each rower holds two oars and must be perfectly synchronized with their partner. Both sets of oars must enter and leave the water at the same time. If either rower is out of sync, you either end up being hit in the kidney with an oar or flipping the boat. As I practiced and bonded with my rowing partner, I learned the mechanics of using the oars in synchrony with my partner, and I fell in love with the sport. Part of the fun came from being in excellent physical condition. The other joy came from working as a pair with another rower. I was unfamiliar with this because swimming is such a solitary activity. Not surprisingly, I also embraced the beauty of skimming across the surface of the water with two oars instead of plowing through the water, swimming with two arms.

My fun seeking didn't stop after rowing. I enjoy most physical challenges, and during the summer of 1997, I climbed Mount Kilimanjaro in Tanzania with a group of eight friends. We were all former collegiate athletes, excited about an adventure and prepared to test our physical stamina. The climb wasn't technical, but our guide warned us that moving slowly, "*pole pole*" in Swahili, was imperative and could save our lives. Ascending to an altitude of 19,000 feet is dangerous if you don't allow time for your body to acclimatize. As we started the seven-day trek, most of my group took off fast, jockeying for the lead position on the trail and challenging each other to keep pace. I heeded the guide's advice and found myself alone at the back of the group, which wasn't a problem for me. I've always been comfortable knowing my limits and not bowing to others' pressure. Reaching the summit wasn't a race, it was a personal challenge. On the third day, as the air grew thinner and the path steeper, we watched a different group descend the mountain carrying a body bag. We stepped aside on the trail to let them pass, and their faces told a story of anguish and tragedy. After that, everyone in our group followed the guide's instructions.

During the last section, I led the climb, setting the pace, taking one step every three seconds. It felt like a snail's pace, but our group made it to the summit safely.

The climb tested my fitness and allowed me to take risks and tackle an adventure on a foreign continent. I kept a journal during the trip and found the experience grueling but enlightening. The hike required patience and trust in our guides. Even though I spent a week without adequate food, hygiene, or sleep, my journal entries were mainly upbeat. I noted the wildlife sightings, the incredible sunsets, and the camaraderie of our group. Despite some struggles during the trip, such as lost luggage and a nasty head cold, I embraced the challenge and grew from the experience. I learned I could handle discomfort and trust myself, my body, and my fitness.

Another form of fun emerged that same year when I changed jobs and began working at The Laurel School, an all-girls school, in Shaker Heights, Ohio (Laurel). After leaving a position as a collegiate swimming coach, Laurel hired me as their director of athletics. During my tenure at Laurel, I helped the school establish a modern athletic culture. One aspect of this was to introduce more sports and show the girls there were many ways to have fun. Fun wasn't simply socializing, hanging out at the mall, or going to the arcade or the movies. Fun could also mean running fast, striking a tennis ball, or practicing with teammates to execute the perfect corner kick in soccer. My goal was to work with the girls to expand their definition of fun to include satisfying physical challenges and competition.

Part of the new culture meant informing the students and parents about my expectations regarding attending school and practice. I instituted a new rule: If a student missed school or practice the day of or the day before a game, they couldn't play in the game. If a player was ill, it was best for them to stay home, convalesce, and return to school and sports when they regained their health. That seemed logical, and I didn't direct my rule at specific players, but to all athletes. Prior to my arrival at Laurel, players often scheduled doctors' appointments during practice time or skipped an early morning study period so they could sleep late on game day. Those students had often played in the game, anyway. The new rule helped athletes prioritize school and connect practice with games. It wasn't a penalty system, but a reward system because the girls wanted to play in the games. Some parents objected, and one student even left the school, but I stood firm and followed through on my expectations. Once the girls realized they improved with practice and playing games was fun, most followed the rules. Very few students missed class or practice because they valued playing in the games. After several seasons, the culture at Laurel changed and athletics became another version of fun. I can still see the proud faces of the girls and feel the uptick in school spirit. I thoroughly enjoyed watching the athletic program blossom under my care, and enjoy hearing about their success today.

People are often curious if I have competed in triathlons. A friend talked me into registering for the *Chicago Sun Times* triathlon when I was 23 or 24; she said it would be fun. My friend was a former swimmer, an avid cyclist, and a regular runner. She encouraged me to join her, even though I had a fear of swimming in open water. "Crazy," most would say, but as a child swimming in Lake Erie, my dad used to scare me with stories about killer carp lurking on the bottom. And during the summer of 1975, when the movie *Jaws* appeared in theaters, my brother often dove under the murky water and yanked on my legs to tease me. I became terrified of swimming in open water and that fear hasn't subsided, even though I know sharks don't live in lakes.

Somehow, in Chicago, I made it through the triathlon with my friend. After starting the swim behind the professional athletes, I exited the water ahead of many competitors. I had survived the 1.5 kilometer swim in Lake Michigan despite my anxiety and unease about the low visibility. Many cyclists passed me on the 40 kilometer bike course, and I limped over the finish line, walking the last stretch of the 10 kilometer run. I felt exhausted from the effort and never entered another triathlon, although many athletes find the sport fun.

Throughout my life, I have remained active and made time to play. Whether it was swimming in my youth, or a mountain bike ride, pickleball game, or stand-up paddle as an adult, I focus on fun. For me, physical activity is essential to my happiness. The joy I feel from playing also brings perspective to my life. I experience routine ups and downs and ride them out with minor frustration and anxiety. Allowing myself time to play brings me a sense of peace and satisfaction in daily life. Plus, I always have something to look forward to.

When parents, coaches, and athletes focus on fun, sports have the power to enhance all lives and bring joy every day. I urge parents to help their child find an activity the child enjoys and looks forward to practicing. Figure out what is fun, and strive to avoid turning children into mini professionals. For coaches, especially those teaching young athletes and beginners, include games and play time along with lessons. Spend time on rules and skills, but allow smiles and laughter to dominate practice time. And for athletes of all ages, find a sport that brings you satisfaction and entices you to play. There is no need to compete; being physically active is its own reward.

Age 10 at the Marietta YMCA.

Age 4 with my brother Pete.

Age 12 having fun with friends (me in the middle).

Age 3 playing in my neighborhood.

Age 8 (back row, second from the left) as the lead in the school play.

Age 8 with Shorty.

CHAPTER
2

LOSING IS PART
OF THE PROCESS

Sports are a great mechanism to learn about making mistakes and handling failure. Many parents want to protect their children from those experiences, but we learn our best lessons by making mistakes. And everyone makes them; it's a fact of life. The sooner children learn this lesson, the better. The world doesn't end when you lose a game. Athletes must learn to accept defeat. That doesn't mean you enjoy losing, but you learn to tolerate it, continue playing, and use it for motivation. Mistakes and failures happen and present an opportunity to learn and grow. These days, there is too much emphasis on winning. Now is a great time to reframe the focus of youth sports. If we return to the process of learning skills, striving for incremental improvement, and having fun, kids will thrive no matter the outcome.

My life competing in amateur sports was about more than winning medals. A victory is temporary, but an athlete's preparation and effort before a game or competition remains. Winning feels important at that moment, but tomorrow, next week, or next year, a different team or individual will prevail. The true reward is what you learn about yourself when you make the journey as an athlete.

This doesn't mean we ignore excellence or downplay a championship. We should applaud record-breaking performances and celebrate milestones. When I had those moments in my swimming career, they were fantastic. At the Pan-Pacific Games in Tokyo in 1985, I recall standing on the podium with a gold medal around my neck, caught up in the moment, trying to remember the words to the National Anthem. I also remember looking up at the scoreboard after swimming a grueling 200-meter backstroke in 1986 and seeing the letters "WR" (an abbreviation for world record) next to my name. With pride, I accepted induction into the International Swimming Hall of Fame in 1998 alongside several other talented athletes. But these were just moments in time. They didn't define me then, and they don't define me now.

In a sport like swimming, one one-hundredth of a second, which is less than the blink of an eye, can separate first and second place. Most competitors don't win. Losing doesn't mean failing, and if we want young athletes to develop robust character and excellent sportsmanship, they must learn to accept a loss and understand it is a normal part of the process. Losing presents an opportunity for improvement. All sports teach this valuable lesson; effort, dedication, and attitude are more important than outcome.

When I was six years old, I finished first place in a Marietta Country Club swimming race that was one width of the pool. My parents saved this epic blue ribbon in a scrapbook; I was off to a good start. During the years I swam at the Marietta YMCA, I earned plenty more red, brown, and purple ribbons for finishing second, fifth or eighth place in races. Like all athletes, I lost more races than I won, but it thrilled me to return home from a swim meet with an array of brightly colored ribbons to decorate my bulletin board. Like most children, with continued practice, I improved because I found the process fun.

Although it may be common sense, it's important to shed light on the learning process as it relates to athletes. It begins with a child showing up for practice because they want to be there. Kids are more inclined to go to practice if they expect it to be fun. Next, there must be regular training or repetition. For example, we must repeat the movement of swinging a baseball bat or a golf club until it becomes second nature, or "muscle memory" as they now call it. Fitness takes time and patience to develop. Athletes must also show a certain amount of dedication to their craft to get better. Dedication flows from a desire to learn and improve. Effort counts, also, and it is essential there is a willingness to do your best, not just during competition, but during practice. Athletes must work to make every exercise, drill, or scrimmage valuable. When these elements come together, an athlete succeeds because they trust and enjoy the process and value the work, even when it's mundane or frustrating. Importantly, a person can control the process, including their own effort, attitude, and dedication. None of us can control what others do on the field or in the pool, so it's best to focus on oneself.

During those formative years at the YMCA, I attended regular swimming practices and listened to my coach. I learned ways to develop my strokes and make flip turns more efficient. Steady training increased my stamina and my race times improved. When I was 11, I changed teams and began swimming at a larger YMCA program in Parkersburg, West Virginia. In Marietta, I had become a big fish in a small pond, and I sought more competition to continue improving. My parents agreed, and we joined a carpool that transported several kids to workouts. The drive took between 20 and 30 minutes, and I would wait on the street corner near my house for a ride. Two teenage boys, Andy and Pat, would pick me up in a sporty Datsun with shag carpet on the dashboard and rock music blaring from the radio. Despite our age difference, they treated me kindly, and I thought of them as my nice big brothers.

Tom Phillips and his wife Jodi coached at the Parkersburg YMCA and created a laid-back playful vibe during practice. The coaches told jokes, and I found this fun and laughed along, even though some punchlines went over my head because most of the other swimmers were high school aged. During practice, we crowded into the narrow lanes of the 25-yard pool. Each lane accommodated six or seven swimmers, and I never wanted to swim last in my lane because the leader might catch up with me. During the first week, I asked Coach Tom about what to do when I caught the swimmer in front of me and my fingertips brushed their toes. He looked at me sternly, but cracked a huge smile. "Swim over them or around them," Tom said. "Whatever you need to do." After that, I didn't hesitate to move ahead to maintain my pace and get my hand on the wall, even if that meant grabbing the ankle of the person in front of me and pulling them backwards to get past. To me, racing the person in the next lane or passing the swimmer in front of me was an opportunity to use my teammates to help me get better. That mindset stuck with me throughout my swimming career: don't let anyone hold you back. I never had an aim of beating a particular person; it was always about racing to see if I could be faster.

My efforts paid off the following year at age 12 when I qualified for my first YMCA national swimming meet. To qualify, athletes must swim faster than a posted time standard for each event. I qualified to swim the 50, 100, and 200-yard freestyle events. This was the first time I would compete against girls of all ages, not just in my age group. At such a young age, it was a victory for me to qualify for a national meet. I was secondarily excited to go to YMCA Nationals because the meet was in Fort Lauderdale, Florida. I was born in Florida and had lived there for the first six months of my life, but didn't remember much. My family had also vacationed in Orlando once when I was eight or nine, but I hadn't been to the coast.

The Parkersburg team traveled together by plane and stayed in a hotel on the beach. My parents went with me, but I roomed with several of my teammates. The swimming pool complex was enormous, the largest I had ever seen, with hundreds of bodies churning through the water during the warm-up period. I had also never seen platform diving towers before, and they loomed over the pool like mythical sentries. Several large YMCA teams dominated the pool deck with their matching sweats, bags, hats, and team banners. Although I didn't swim fast enough to qualify for the finals in my races, it thrilled me to be there, and I had a ton of fun.

I also learned something about swimmers during that meet, and I chuckle every time I recall the incident involving an older teammate. He was 17 or 18 years old and had lots of body hair. It was his first YMCA nationals too, and he shaved his entire body before his race. It was my first exposure to shaving. I hadn't reached puberty yet and knew nothing about it, how swimmers let their arm and leg hair grow during the season and shave it off when they taper their training and peak for a big meet. [2] My teammate shaved his arms, legs, back, and chest and then jumped into the warm Atlantic Ocean to see how it felt with smooth skin. I still envision him as he dashed across the sand, dove into the water, only to sprint back out, squealing and screeching. We all learned it hurts to immerse your body in saltwater immediately after shaving.

After those first YMCA Nationals, I continued to swim on the Parkersburg YMCA team for a few more years. I competed in local and regional meets, and returned to YMCA Nationals three more times from 1979 to 1981. Although I often swam the backstroke events in smaller meets, I didn't consider myself a backstroker. Freestyle and butterfly were my main events, and I enjoyed swimming the individual medley, which requires all four strokes in one race. I don't remember when I added more backstroke to my training, but I have a hunch I added more because I grew weary of staring at the black line on the bottom of the pool. Few sports involve the level of sensory deprivation as swimming. Equivalents might include running on a treadmill or cycling on a stationary bike while looking at a blank wall and without hearing music. By turning onto my back, I broadened my view to include the ceiling of the

---

2 Tapering means reducing training and resting one's body to prepare for optimal performance.

YMCA with its fluorescent lights, air ducts, and backstroke flags at each end of the pool.

By 1981, at age 15, I swam my best times in the 100-yard freestyle (sixth place), 200-yard freestyle (seventh place), and 100-yard butterfly (sixth place) at the spring YMCA Nationals. Although I didn't win, those times qualified me for the United States Swimming National Junior Olympics (NJOs), a national competition open to swimmers aged 18 and under. Qualifying for NJOs thrilled me because it gave me the opportunity to race against the top junior swimmers in the country. The YMCA Nationals were only open to YMCA members, and I knew there were thousands of swimmers in the United States who competed for club teams, not the YMCA.

I continued to improve, and in June 1984, at age 18, I qualified as a member of the United States Olympic team. I was to swim the 100-meter backstroke and the medley relay in the Los Angeles Olympics. Becoming an Olympian was exciting, but also nerve-racking. I was keenly aware of the stress and relevance of the Games to the athletes who had been denied the chance to compete in 1980. Because of the Soviet Union's invasion of Afghanistan, the United States and several other countries boycotted the 1980 Olympics in Moscow. I wanted to do my best while also enjoying the full Los Angeles Olympic experience. Since I did not compete on the first or second day of the Games, I joined several teammates, along with thousands of athletes from other countries, in the Coliseum for the opening ceremonies. Even though the ceremony required standing for hours in the scorching sun, it was incredibly inspiring to take part in the athletes' parade and witness the lighting of the Olympic flame. I felt very proud to represent my hometown and my country.

Living in a dormitory in the athletes' village at the University of Southern California produced its own blend of fun and mischief, almost like starting college again. Most of the U.S. team lived in the same dorm, so it created opportunities to interact with athletes from other sports. After wandering the Olympic Village one day, I rode the elevator with basketball player Michael Jordan and gymnast Mary Lou Retton. [3] I pinched myself as we made our way up to the dorms; me, an unknown swimmer flanked by tall, muscular Michael and petite pixie, Mary Lou. I imagine we were a humorous sight, the epitome of small, medium, and large.

With a staggered schedule of competitive events at the Olympics, some athletes in our dorm slept until noon while others awakened before dawn to prepare for their races. The cafeteria stayed open 24 hours a day, and the clanging of dishes and chatter of languages sounded like fifth grade band practice. The swimming team had specific rules and a curfew, and I typically went to bed early, but we often saw other athletes get picked up in limousines to attend parties or special events in Los Angeles. Many athletes felt jubilant with the atmosphere after missing the 1980 Olympics. Considering all the distractions, it's a miracle anyone could focus on competing.

When the day arrived for me to race in the 100-meter backstroke, it shocked me to swim in front of a huge, screaming crowd instead of just friends and parents in the bleachers. Although I had been to the competition pool for training and had cheered for the U.S. team during their events on the previous days, the enormity of it all struck me at that moment. In the swim stadium, I felt the expectations of everyone watching. My stomach turned somersaults and, standing in my bathing suit, I could see my heart beating beneath my skin. It was the first time I felt any external pressure to perform. It was the Olympics!

The 100 backstroke was my race to win. I had finished first in the event at the Olympic trials. When I qualified first in the Olympic preliminaries in Los Angeles, I believed people expected me to win. Even I expected myself to win, but someone else won the race that

---

3 Coincidentally, I have a connection to both athletes, although I do not know them personally. Michael Jordan played basketball at the University of North Carolina (UNC) when I swam for UNC. We ate meals at the same training table. Mary Lou Retton grew up in Fairmont, West Virginia, also in Appalachia, about forty-five minutes from my hometown, Marietta, Ohio.

day. My teammate Theresa Andrews swam better, and I finished second. I did nothing wrong during the race, managing a good start, a steady first 50 meters, and a solid turn at the wall. What differed from the Olympic Trials was my speed and power during the second half of the race. I didn't have that burst of energy or higher gear to finish strong. When my hand touched the wall, I knew the race would be close. Swimming backstroke, you can shift your eyes and quickly glance to the side towards your competitors, but with variations in arm length and arm speed it's almost impossible to know your placing until the end. When I saw the scoreboard, my heart sank. I had lost by eight one-hundredths of a second. [4] For a moment, I felt despondent. I thought I'd swim faster. I quickly plastered a smile on my face and congratulated Theresa. When I pulled myself out of the pool, although I felt deflated, the Olympic Games and life continued.

Losing didn't bother me as much as failing to focus and not swimming my best race. Although most people don't believe me, I was truly happy at that moment. I was an Olympian who had just won a silver medal, and we had placed first and second for the United States. I showed good sportsmanship, not because I was conscious of that, but because I had practiced it. Being a good sport and accepting defeat had been ingrained and normalized in my life. This was a moment in time, not the end of the world. As a consolation, a few days later, I swam the backstroke leg in the preliminary heats of the medley relay, which later won a gold medal. Although I didn't get to be a direct part of that win because I didn't swim in the final, the International Olympic Committee later awarded me a gold medal for contributing to the United States' victory in that event.

It is common for some athletes to become overwhelmed at the Olympic Games and perform terribly. Many become mentally intimidated by the magnitude of the event or believe the Olympics mean *everything*. For me, in the grand scheme of things, the

---

4 The winner, Theresa Andrews, swam a time of 1:02.55 in the 100-meter backstroke, and I finished second with a time of 1:02.63.

Olympic Games were just another swim meet. Like all the meets before, the Olympics were an opportunity to test myself and have fun. My life wasn't over because I didn't win. I had parents and friends who loved me, and I knew my life would continue, no matter the outcome. Swimming was an integral part of my life. I loved the sport and looked ahead to more training, future races, and the opportunity to be better.

The entire 1984 Olympic experience was incredible, and I felt proud to represent my country and my hometown. When I returned to Marietta, Ohio, a welcoming parade organized in my honor surprised me. As my flight descended into the local airport, we circled the tiny airstrip while the pilot addressed us passengers: "We have a local celebrity on board, Betsy Mitchell. Congratulations on your performance at the Olympics." I peered out the window of the 16-seat airplane at the crowd of 100 gathered near the tarmac. When we deplaned and walked outside down the steps, my parents and best friend Gretchen greeted me with hugs. I rode in my parents' car downtown and climbed aboard a trailer decorated in red, white, and blue ribbons and bows. As the parade began, a marching band led the way. I waved to the crowd and gazed at the streets lined with thousands of people. Colorful balloons, crepe paper streamers, and homemade signs decorated the street. Only 12,000 people lived in Marietta, Ohio, and it felt like the whole town had come out to cheer for me and express their congratulations. My friends and neighbors didn't care that I had finished second in the race; they were simply excited that someone from Marietta, Ohio, was an Olympian. As their first hometown Olympian, I was happy, too. When the parade stopped several blocks later, I climbed the courthouse steps and listened to speeches from the mayor and city council members. I spoke briefly and thanked everyone for coming and cheering for me.

I have wonderful memories of my teammates, the Olympic Village, and the excitement of the LA Games. My hard work had paid off. Without the process of dedicated training and effort, I would never have had a chance for this outcome. In that moment, I realized being a winner meant being content with myself, confident in my abilities, and proud of the work I had done.

I continued to train and race for four more years until the 1988 Olympics. There, in Seoul, South Korea, with a few exceptions, the East German women dominated the swimming events at those Games. We felt certain their athletes used performance-enhancing drugs, but that wouldn't be my excuse. I wanted to race and did my best to ignore their deep voices, pronounced Adam's apples, and angular jaw lines. And I knew we could beat them because in December 1985 at the U.S. Swimming Open meet in Austin, Texas, I had bested Cornelia Sirch, the world record holder and dominant East German backstroker. At that international meet, I had won both the 100 and 200-meter backstrokes and set American records for my performances. Three years later in Seoul, 1985 seemed like a lifetime ago. As a 22-year-old at the 1988 Games, I was not the same person or swimmer, and unlike the 1984 Games, nobody expected me to win any events.

Few would remember it, but I was fourth in the 100-meter backstroke final at the Seoul Olympics, missing the podium and a medal. [5] Unfortunately, my best swims were never at the Olympics, although I gave it everything I had. It was just another race, and I was fourth best on that day. Naturally, it was disappointing to not swim the way I had prepared, but some days are like that and life goes on. I earned a silver medal at those 1988 Games in the medley relay. Just as in Los Angeles in 1984, I swam the backstroke leg in the preliminary heats. In the finals of the medley relay, the United States team placed second.

Although I loved swimming the 100-meter backstroke, during the summer of 1988, my heart felt empty. I didn't want to be in Seoul

---

5 Kristin Otto of the German Democratic Republic (GDR) finished first with a time of 1:00.89. Krisztina Egerszegi of Hungary finished second with a time of 1:01.56, and Cornelia Sirch of the GDR finished third with a time of 1:01.57. I finished fourth with a time of 1:02.71.

and swimming no longer felt fun. I was ready to leave the sport behind and move on with my life, but as an older member of the team and one of the leaders, I knew I couldn't give up. I felt obligated to compete and shepherd the younger swimmers on their journey. Four years prior, at my first Olympics, I had been that person who needed a friend, some encouragement, and a bit of advice. I went to Seoul to help the team and learned from my experience that I wanted to coach. By cheering for the team, spending time with friends, and experiencing the city of Seoul with my family, I enjoyed the trip. Even though I felt done with swimming, I still believed winning was about my attitude, not about a result or outcome.

Much like beauty, success is personal, and definitions of success vary from person to person. Even when an athlete doesn't win, they can find satisfaction in some aspect of their performance. In swimming, it can easily be their time, effort, or placing. For me, the process of consistent training fed my desire to test my physical limits and swim faster. At the 1988 Olympics, I achieved success through my effort and refusal to give up.

For me, society's idea of success, a huge paycheck or fame, didn't resonate. I believed working diligently to achieve a goal, even if you came up short, was success. If you love what you're doing, keep striving. I was proud to compete in Seoul, but knew my swimming career was complete. After returning to the United States, I immediately translated my love of the sport to becoming a swimming coach. It was time to share what I had learned with others.

Today, as an athletic director, I measure the success of a collegiate athletic program by assessing the quality of the experience of the students. I help my school focus on the process of training and working as a team, challenging our athletes to improve. In return, these student-athletes build a connection with the university and their teammates. Every day, they learn through trial and error in the "athletic laboratory," which is life in a nutshell. Most of the athletes

I work with have learned you can be a winner and feel successful even when you don't win.

We must remind our children that it's okay to make mistakes, lose, and fail. One can play their best and not win. It's a normal part of life. Perhaps your daughter plays goalkeeper in soccer. She is human and cannot block every shot, but if she's trying her best, she will learn from the challenge. Basketball player Michael Jordan has spoken about the number of shots he missed during his career, yet "you can't score any points unless you shoot." The same is true in baseball, where players often strike out, yet "you can't hit the ball unless you swing," and players often swing and miss. The sooner kids learn to accept failure as part of the process of improving, the better. Failure is an important life skill that fosters perseverance. Finally, athletes must be humble. A game is just a game, to be played hard, enjoyed, and then left behind.

I urge parents to support their kids by staying positive, applauding effort, and ignoring the win-loss records of the team. Coaches can do the same by encouraging their players and keeping the focus on learning new skills and incremental improvement. Athletes benefit most when they concentrate on what they can control: going to practice, working hard, and maintaining a positive attitude. Together, we can reframe the focus of amateur sports so that we play and have fun, regardless of whether we win or lose. The true reward isn't a medal, trophy, or title. Participation, effort, and striving to improve oneself are the prize. The same logic applies to academics and grades. It's nice to receive A's, but learning the material, tapping curiosity, and understanding a different perspective is the reward. The process, not the outcome, is what changes us and improves us as people.

Age 17 after Mercersburg Academmy's
dual meet loss to Mission Viejo High School.

1984 Olympic Games, silver medal
in the 100-meter backstroke.

Age 19, second place
to Cornelia Sirch.
I later broke her world
record at age 20.

CHAPTER
3

INTRINSIC MOTIVATION MATTERS

The concept of amateurism is deeply connected to motivation, specifically internal or intrinsic motivation. I don't have a Ph.D., and I'm not a psychologist or social scientist, but I am an athlete, educator, and leader. The power of internal motivation comes from the heart; it is personal and sustainable. Motivation drives the process of incremental improvement, allowing athletes to strive to be better and develop self-respect. You can lose the game, but still succeed, and you don't expect any reward other than the joy of competing.

In my early days as an age-group swimmer in Ohio, I didn't win many races, especially at first. In the beginning, I earned a few blue ribbons for first place, but the bulk of my satisfaction came from being with friends, challenging myself, and lowering my times. I considered any improvement in my performance a victory.

My concern is that young athletes today have lost touch with intrinsic motivation; why they play. Some kids participate in sports because they love the game or thrive on competition, but others play to please their parents or build their resume. Unfortunately, some kids don't have a choice about what or whether to play; their parents mandate sports. And it breaks my heart to see children immediately look at their parents' reaction during a game to determine whether the child is performing well. I feel these are the wrong reasons to play. Focusing on external rewards or outcomes when athletes are young and impressionable is dangerous. The process of improvement is infinitely more valuable for youth; wanting to get better rather than wanting to win or earn a reward. It is also misguided for young children to focus on or expect monetary rewards or college scholarship opportunities. Those may come, but playing and learning are more important.

The National Collegiate Athletic Association (NCAA) governs much of college sports in the United States. Colleges and universities are members of the NCAA, which divides schools into three divisions. The larger schools comprise Division I and offer athletic scholarships to student-athletes. Division II schools provide mostly partial athletic scholarships, while Division III schools only offer academic scholarships and need-based financial aid. The odds of becoming an NCAA Division I scholarship athlete are slim, and the chances of becoming a professional athlete are even smaller. Parents can encourage and support their kids by focusing on the moment and not the future. I consider myself fortunate for the way my parents raised me. They got it right; any focus on the future concerned my education, not swimming.

Unfortunately, many parents live vicariously through their children. This pressure causes parents to urge their children to win rather than have fun or learn skills and fair play. I've seen the stress of this dynamic played out many times. Children should feel good about playing sports rather than worrying about disappointing their parents. If a family spends their hard-earned money on elite travel teams, personal trainers, and private lessons, the stakes increase for both parents and children, especially when a family spends money on sports but doesn't save for future educational expenses. After doling out hundreds or thousands of dollars, parents expect their kids to win and children feel pressure to continue playing, even if they don't want to. This whole dynamic creates stress and anxiety for a family unless the child is self-motivated. In that situation, a child plays because they love the game, and they compete because they thrive on racing or performing.

I experienced a different upbringing growing up in the 1970s. I had more freedom and more time for unstructured play. Children today are over-scheduled and their parents are often overly involved, hovering around their children, asking them why they missed a shot or dropped the ball. My parents literally got out of my way, but helped behind the scenes and at home. After a race, most swimmers consult with their coach and recap the event, discussing what went well and where to improve. My parents had the sense to let the coach advise me and allow me to digest the information and use it at my discretion. When we got home, we didn't rehash the swimming meet or discuss strategies to improve. They recognized my motivation and refrained from adding significance or pressure to my hobby. Many parents today attempt to coach from the sidelines during a game or in the car on the way home. Most kids don't need additional pressure and only need to hear sports advice from their coach. Parents must recognize their role as listeners who support their child.

Another major difference about my upbringing was my parents expected me to contribute as a family member with daily and weekly chores. I remember the 1970s being a time when people did their own landscaping, painting, window washing, and housecleaning. I mowed the lawn during the summer, raked leaves in the fall, and shoveled snow during the winter. One summer, my parents insisted my brother and I clear the backyard for a new patio. Of course, I would have preferred to sleep late, hang out with my friends, or do almost anything else, but I didn't. I may have been sassy and complained about the job, but I wasn't defiant. My brother and I spent a significant part of that summer removing all the grass and bushes from our backyard by hand. We dug with shovels and clawed the earth with hoes to clear the greenery. When our yard was bare, we raked the dirt until it was nearly flat, and laid the brick for the new patio. Unless you live on a farm or ranch, kids don't do this type of labor anymore. For me, working hard and contributing to the family gave me a feeling of satisfaction. When we completed the task, I felt confident in my ability to do the work.

Most athletic endeavors are arduous. Sports take hours, weeks, months, and years of practice and training to master. The possibility of injuries is ever present. Sometimes improvement arrives at a snail's pace, but if you find the process fun, or find value in your efforts, it's worthwhile. Swimming is a tough sport. Most of the time, you're alone with your thoughts, which leaves plenty of room for pity, self-doubt, or fear of missing out to creep in. But the properly motivated athlete can overcome negative self-talk. For me, the schedule, repetition, physicality, and structure of swimming fit my personality. The experience was entirely mine, not my parents', coaches', or teammates'.

After I had joined the larger YMCA swimming program in Parkersburg, West Virginia, I had to travel farther to get to practice. This wasn't a problem for me because I wanted to be in the pool. After a brief time, my coach suggested I attend some morning workouts before school. I was only 12, but I wanted to go so I could train and get faster. My dad agreed to drive me early in the mornings, but he told me, "Get yourself up. This is your thing." And he meant it. I used an alarm clock, and if I overslept, my parents didn't wake me. No one forced me to swim. Nobody yelled at me or put unrealistic demands on me. And as a 12-year-old, the thought of swimming in college had never crossed my mind. What motivated me was my relentless internal drive to improve.

When I quit swimming for a week during ninth grade, I went back to the pool because I realized I loved the sport. My parents didn't make me return, but my dad had shared his wisdom with me. "Evaluate at the end of the season," he told me. "Not in the middle." He explained that no matter the challenge, sometimes you hit a wall and want to give up. It happens to everybody. He felt it was important that I stick it out and wait to assess the situation when my emotions were more settled. I agreed then, and I still agree. Unless an athlete is in danger and needs to take immediate action, waiting to decide makes sense. When I returned to the pool, I knew it was the right choice for me. If I hadn't thrived upon training and competing, leaving the sport or adjusting my practice schedule would have been the better option.

Two years later, at age 15, with support from my parents, I enrolled at the Mercersburg Academy for my junior and senior years of high school. Mercersburg is a college preparatory school in southern Pennsylvania. I felt ready for more challenges both in school and in swimming; my parents agreed. After researching and touring a few schools in Florida and some closer to home, I chose Mercersburg. My parents and I discussed the move because leaving home would disrupt the family dynamic. My brother, a senior in high school at the time, was angry because his little sister planned to move out of the house before him. As the older child, he expected to leave home first. He got over it, but we endured a few tense weeks. From a swimming standpoint, attending Mercersburg wasn't a problem because I had never swum for my high school team. Marietta High School's swimming program was less rigorous than my training at the Parkersburg YMCA. This also allowed my brother to be the standout local high school swimmer of the family.

Mercersburg Academy reminded me of a small college with multiple classroom buildings, an enormous library, and friendly people. The beautiful campus included brick buildings and broad lawns. The spire of the chapel rose high above the trees. John Trembley, Mercersburg's swimming coach (we called him "JT"), exuded confidence when he met me, and immediately drew me in with his gregarious personality. He was a standout swimmer in the 1970s at the University of Tennessee. When I met him, he even complimented the flexibility in my feet and ankles.

As a coach, JT made me feel like a part of the team from day one. Although I didn't know any of the other swimmers at Mercersburg, the team had a reputation for excellence. I quickly got to know my teammates, but never lived in the cool girls' dorm. Content with my lack of popularity, I preferred a quieter existence where I focused on classwork and showed up at practice to work hard and improve my swimming. My experience of enrolling at Mercersburg, spreading my wings, and assuming responsibility for my actions, opened my eyes to what the world could be. I had always been a go-getter, adventurous, and curious about new things. The move was consistent with my personality, and I felt ready for the challenge.

Although it thrilled me to face a new adventure at Mercersburg, it was quite a change to live away from my parents at a boarding school. I felt nervous but believed I could do it. When I moved into the on-campus housing, I met the main dormitory "mom," Debbie Rutherford, a Spanish teacher living on campus. I felt an immediate connection with her because she was born in Muncie, Indiana, like my mom. I also met Miss Eadie, the hall "mom" on the second floor where I roomed. She was a chemistry teacher and the cross-country coach. With her wiry frame, toned calves, and long blonde ponytail, she exuded cool "big sister" vibes, and I knew I would like her. When we spoke, I eagerly listened to Miss Eadie's advice and cared about what she thought.

For students who lived on campus, lunch and dinner were served family-style in a sit-down communal dining hall. Although the food at the time was mediocre, we rotated tables regularly, with faculty and students eating together. This wasn't a problem for me as I felt comfortable conversing with my parents and other adults. Breakfast became a favorite meal because I stuffed myself with Captain Crunch cereal and visited the waffle-making station as often as possible. I adjusted to using the bathroom down the hall and learned to do my laundry. For the first time, I had a roommate, Becky. She was from rural Pennsylvania and was not an athlete, but we were from similar small towns and developed a good relationship. There wasn't a television in our room, and personal computers, tablets, and cell phones did not yet exist. We often joined others in the common area to watch "M*A*S*H," "Cheers," or movies on the weekends. Becky and I also attended sporting events on campus, like field hockey and baseball, and cheered for our home team during those games. I spent weekends swimming, sleeping, and doing homework. I lived a scheduled life from morning to evening and benefited from the structure. Attending Mercersburg empowered me to flex the muscle of independence within a safe, organized framework.

Mercersburg also required me to change my training. The girls' swimming team practiced with the boys and JT assigned our lanes according to speed or stroke, not gender. This was like the YMCA, but the competition was much tougher. When I worked hard to lead my lane, the boys always seemed faster. This increased the intensity of the workouts as we swam more yards per day at faster intervals. [6] Several days each week, JT also had us work out in the gym. They call this "dry land" training, and we did a circuit of weights, jumps, stretch bands, and abdominal (now called core) exercises. The first few weeks of dry land training punished my muscles, given that in the past I had done little strength training. My arms and legs ached, and I felt exhausted; however, the team and the new schedule energized me.

I swam well as a member of the Mercersburg team and continued to improve my times. In a moment of reflection during the spring of my junior year, I realized I couldn't return to the Parkersburg YMCA. I had outgrown their program and I discussed my thoughts with my parents as we investigated different training options. After careful consideration of location and costs, my parents agreed I could spend each of my last two summers of high school in Cincinnati, Ohio training with the Cincinnati Pepsi Marlins. Cincinnati is about three and one-half hours west of Marietta. I had been there previously for swimming meets and knew the team had an exceptionally competitive program. During those summers, I lived

---

6 An interval is an amount of time allotted to swim a specific distance. If the interval is 45 seconds for each 50 yards, if you swim the distance in 35 seconds, you would get 10 seconds of rest before starting the next interval.

with two different families, the Lechners and the Kreigers. Both had rented apartments and moved to Cincinnati because their daughters were chasing the same dream of making the Olympic team. These girls and I benefitted by training with other world-class swimmers. Again, this was my choice, and my parents supported the decision, even though it meant our family continued to live apart.

Training in Cincinnati allowed me to test my abilities. It was there where I transitioned from junior level meets (for swimmers aged 18 and under) to senior meets (open to all ages). During the summer of 1982 at 16, I finished second in the 100-meter backstroke at my first U.S. National Swimming Championships in Indianapolis. To my surprise, I earned Rookie of the Meet honors, qualifying for a place on the USA-USSR (Union of Soviet Socialist Republics) dual meet team. The United States hosted the dual meet in Knoxville, Tennessee, as part of the World's Fair, and it was my first national team experience. This opportunity showed me that if I swam fast, U.S. Swimming could select me to compete on an even larger scale. It thrilled me to be a part of Team USA, and many of my U.S. teammates were 1980 Olympic Team members. They wanted a chance to beat the Russians. The United States prevailed over the Soviet Union, 223-156 in the dual meet, and I performed well, finishing third in the 100-meter backstroke, and fifth in both the 200-meter backstroke and 100-meter butterfly.

Meeting different coaches and older swimmers motivated me to consider swimming in college. When I was a senior in high school, I traveled on recruiting trips to Arizona State University, Southern Methodist University, The University of Texas at Austin, and The University of North Carolina in Chapel Hill (UNC). My Mercersburg guidance counselor recommended UNC as the "best," and my parents let me decide. They trusted I would make an educated and thoughtful choice. I opted for UNC because it was a smaller school and closer to home. I didn't want to overextend myself and the choice suited my tendency to take small steps and only "bite off what I thought I could chew." Another key factor in my decision was Sue Walsh, a 1980 Olympian and the American record holder in the 100 backstroke. She attended UNC and that meant we would be teammates. To improve, I needed to train with the best.

In the fall of 1983, I attended UNC on a full athletic scholarship. Because I had previously attended Mercersburg and lived away from home, I made a smooth transition to college life, moving into my dorm, meeting my new roommate Amy, and adjusting to a new schedule. As a freshman at the NCAA National Swimming Championships in March 1984, I finished third in the 100-yard backstroke. I felt disappointed about not winning the race, but not winning ended up being one of the best things that happened to me. The Olympic Games were only a few months away, and I felt I could swim faster. I wanted to be a part of the U.S. team and knew I had to change my training to earn a spot on the Olympic team.

Although playing or competing on a team can be a huge motivator, an athlete must have the personal drive to show up every day, work hard, and maintain a positive attitude. Unfortunately, UNC was not optimal for me. After my freshman year, I transferred to The University of Texas at Austin (UT) and joined the Longhorns team, training with Richard Quick, another coach who exuded energy and confidence. The year before, when I had made my initial college decision, I told Richard I had chosen UNC. He was respectful of my choice and wished me well, but told me there was always a place for me in Austin. I appreciated his friendly demeanor and positive attitude, and his position of support led me back to Texas one year later.

While at Texas, I began to understand the significance of internal motivation. On weekday afternoons, our women's team would gather on the pool deck before a practice session. Richard often rolled out the chalkboard, and our usually jovial group would fall silent. Our smiles turned to frowns and heavy sighs filled the damp air as Richard reviewed the days' workout. We would warm up in the pool for 1,000 yards, kick a set, and then proceed to the meat of the workout: the main set. The team would release a collective groan when Richard flipped the chalkboard over, revealing the other side with a set that was six to eight thousand yards. At those moments, I had to look deep inside my heart and remind myself why I was there and what I wanted to accomplish. Before those brutal sets, I had to prepare mentally for the challenge. Looking back, I understand that enjoying and trusting the process allowed me to embrace training and ultimately improve through dedication and hard work. The reward wasn't money or a prize; it was the bolstering of self-confidence, proving to myself I could do it, and the satisfaction of completing the task.

Today, our culture has morphed collegiate and amateur sports into entertainment. This distorts the original reason for playing sports, for fun and personal satisfaction. Unfortunately, when we focus on money, titles, or prizes as the goal rather than the character of our accomplishments, we risk destroying athletes' internal drive and motivation. The prospect of compensation also creates pressure to perform and win at all costs. I believe those types of external factors cannot support healthy development, particularly in children. Instead, playing sports creates stress and anxiety instead of smiles and laughter. The external rewards that often drive sports today are inferior in terms of fun, learning, and character development. It's simple; the money isn't worth the sacrifice of athletes' motivation.

We must strive to avoid overinvestment by parents in their children's sports and activities. The intersection of parents' hopes and dreams can interfere with a young athlete's own journey of self-discovery. Pressure to perform and win creates unnecessary angst in our kids. A parent's job is to provide guidance and support, not to control every facet of a child's life. I'm lucky because I have self-directed my entire career. My parents listened to my concerns and provided unconditional love, but didn't steer the ship. They also allowed me to make decisions and take responsibility for my choices and achievements. I made mistakes, but I gained confidence and self-respect. Best of all, I felt empowered to dictate the plan for my life and change course when ready for a new challenge.

This type of parental guidance fosters personal growth in young athletes. It also allows a child to experience satisfaction that is sustainable. Most of us will never be professional athletes and a majority will not earn a college athletic scholarship. For intrinsically motivated kids, their desire to play doesn't burn out quickly and the lessons they learn remain for a lifetime. For many, the spotlight of participating in sports eventually fades. The spotlight faded for me, but I felt secure about everything I had learned along the way.

In 1988, after the completion of my collegiate swimming career, my internal motivation to train and improve faltered. I no longer found swimming fun. Even though I had qualified for the Seoul Olympics, my body was tired and I had lost the drive to compete. I went to the 1988 Games because I was supposed to be there. As one of the dominant U.S. females in swimming, I attended out of obligation, but I wasn't happy. No surprise, I swam poorly, which isn't as important as not wanting to be there. I was ready to move on with my life and do other things.

Intrinsic motivation carried me through the ups and downs of swimming, and the same type of drive helped in other areas of my life. For example, when I took the head coaching position at Dartmouth in 1991, the job required that I do everything. I didn't have a secretary or an assistant, so I coached, recruited, and worked to develop my student athletes. If the team was going to get better, it was my responsibility, and I relished that challenge. Every day, I made a list of high school students to call about swimming and studying at Dartmouth. I made cold calls and introduced myself, the program, and the school, hoping for an opportunity to coax motivated athletes to Hanover, New Hampshire. Instead of waiting for someone to direct me or tell me what to do, I just did it.

Whether one is studying to earn a college degree, striving for a promotion at work, or completing an ironman triathlon, the desire to succeed is half the battle. Major employers have found that the internal drive exhibited by former athletes is a key asset and seek this when hiring employees. Company executives know athletes take pride in their work, have a tireless work ethic, and find satisfaction in a job done well. During my years of swimming, I learned what needed to be done to improve, and made it happen. Intrinsic motivation propelled me to succeed in the swimming pool, in the classroom, and in my career.

I marvel when I see a child choose their own path and take the lead in pursuing their interests. When a child says, "I want to do this," they take responsibility for their actions and learn self-direction. Letting kids make their own choices and mistakes builds confidence as long as parents provide love and support, not anger and condemnation. When a child's intrinsic motivation drives their behavior, they are more likely to find satisfaction in their effort and success in the outcome. When parents guide but don't direct, they allow space for their children to develop self-worth. Today, with television and social media accessible at every turn, it's more difficult for young athletes to disregard external rewards, but I still think it's possible. Parents must be realistic and not push their children to pursue activities that make their kids unhappy. Children need time and space to discover and pursue their own interests.

Training in Mission Viejo, California before the 1984 Olympics.

My 1984 Olympic Games identification card.

Games of the
XXIIrd Olympiad
Los Angeles 1984

Jeux de la
XXIIIème Olympiade
Los Angeles 1984

F

BETSY MITCHELL
COMPETITOR
UNITED STATES

1 2 8

At the 1984 Olympics, warming up before the preliminary heats of the 100-meter backstroke at the University of Southern California pool with Coach Gambril.

45

Proud of winning the silver medal in the 100-meter backstroke at the 1984 Olympics.

The 1984 Olympic swimming venue in Los Angeles.

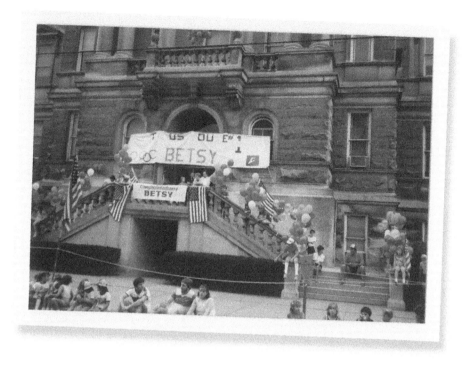

Homecoming parade through town to the courthouse steps in Marietta, Ohio after the 1984 Olympics.

CHAPTER
4

COMPETE, DON'T COMPARE

Each of us is unique. That is why it's best not to compare ourselves to others. This message is especially important to instill in children. Children grow, mature, and learn at different rates. In athletics, they progress at different paces. The fastest runner in a first-grade class may not be the fastest runner by the fourth grade. The tallest student in sixth grade may be one of the shorter students by the eighth grade. It takes time for children to find their way and learn new skills. Just because a child is not the best doesn't mean they should give up. If they love what they're doing, parents should encourage them to keep striving.

Swimming is a wonderful sport for young athletes to focus on their individual achievements because they're racing against the clock. When I was eight, I sometimes had to compete in the 10-and-under category at a swimming meet because that was the youngest age group available. My competitors and I differed in strength and fitness, but I didn't let that bother me. My purpose was to race and improve my times.

But I wasn't always that confident. In fourth grade, I struggled to see the chalkboard at school and my doctor fitted me with glasses.

Few children wore eyeglasses at such a young age, and I felt self-conscious about it. My vision problems also caused difficulty in the pool because I couldn't see the pace clock very well. I discovered later that the sweeping hand of the clock, its steady movement around the clock face, was much easier to follow than square digital numbers. This was a minor setback for me, certainly not one that kept me from working hard. I took my cues from swimmers in the lanes next to me and pushed off the wall when they did. If I was behind, I sprinted to catch up to them before the first flip turn. As a bonus, learning to use a pace clock benefited me at school. Math lessons were easier because I had used the clock to count intervals and track the repetitions of each set and combinations of laps.

When I was 11, I learned a fundamental lesson about the power of competing and not comparing. For several years, I had raced against a talented young swimmer from West Virginia named Julie. She was a year older than me, and it seemed like every time I raced against her, I would finish second, and she would finish first. It didn't matter which event we had swum. During one meet, the last race was a 100-yard freestyle. I had finished second to Julie in all my previous races that day, and I told my dad before the event, "I can't beat her because she has swum 1:04 and my best is only 1:05." My dad looked at me and shook his head. "Don't tell me you can't beat her," he said. Certainly, he was right. I was comparing myself to Julie and focusing on the outcome instead of preparing to compete. In my young mind, I had already lost the race. After the actual race, I finished second with a time of 1:07 and Julie won by swimming 1:06. It's easy to say it now, but if I had competed and swum even close to my best time, I could have won that race. But I didn't do that. I had compared myself to Julie, and she beat me.

A similar situation happened a few years later as a member of the Parkersburg YMCA team. My older teammate Kim was the designated female backstroker on the team. At swim meets, including the YMCA national meet, she always swam the backstroke leg of the medley relay because she had been consistently faster than me in backstroke. I swam the butterfly leg and was fine with that until the day I became the better backstroker. By age 14, I had improved dramatically and began swimming faster than Kim. Although she was older, my times were better.

After learning that lesson, during future competitions, I no longer dwelled on the age, experience, or previous best times of other swimmers. I focused on my race and didn't compare myself to others. As a child, I had never looked up to or idolized anyone in sports. I was blissfully unaware of others. Of course, record-setting performances had impressed me, but I swam to pursue my own goals. I didn't want to be as fast as another swimmer. I wanted to be the fastest.

In the summer of 1981, I was 15 and had qualified for the U.S. Swimming National Junior Olympics (NJOs) meet in Mission Viejo, California. I knew very little about the meet other than it was a chance to race against the top swimmers aged 18 and under in the country. Coach Tom at the Parkersburg YMCA suggested I go to test myself against tougher competition. I felt conflicted because my family had planned to visit the Grand Canyon with a rafting trip on the Colorado River during that summer. I wanted to be with my family on that adventure, but I also wanted to challenge myself in the pool. If I attended NJOs, it would disrupt my family's vacation because Coach Tom could not travel with me to California for the meet. Needing a chaperone, I discussed the predicament with my parents. They agreed I could go to NJOs with my mom, and my dad and brother would enjoy the Grand Canyon. It was the first time my family split our vacation because of swimming, and I'm grateful for my mom's support.

Not only did my mom accompany me, but the situation forced her to step in as my coach. On the crowded pool deck in Southern California, a coaches' lanyard dangling around her neck, my mom learned how to use a stopwatch to help me warm up for the backstroke events. If you've ever watched the warm-up period at a large swimming meet, you'll agree it looks like controlled chaos. Coaches on the pool deck shout and whistle at their athletes packed into the lanes. You swim like a tight school of fish in a tank, one person's fingertips touching the toes of the person in front of them. My mom jostled for position with the other coaches near the edge of the pool as I explained how to take my split times during warm-up. She timed me as I swam 50-meter increments in the pool so I could determine my speed and pacing.

Plenty of the swimmers had qualified for the meet with faster times than mine, but I kept my focus on my warm-up and my races. When I swam the finals of the 200-meter backstroke, I startled myself and finished in first. (I had already placed second in the 100-meter backstroke the previous day.) My mom was also stunned at my performance and the only thing I remember her asking was, "What do we do now?" In true swimmer fashion, I said, "Let's go eat!" Even though I had swum personal best times at the meet and placed well, I had missed an incredible rafting trip. When my dad and brother told me about it, I understood, if I wanted to keep swimming and pursue my passion, the future might involve more trade-offs and tough decisions.

One year later, during the summer of 1982, I qualified for the U.S. Swimming Senior Nationals, the top meet in the country. The Cincinnati team traveled to Indianapolis for the opportunity to race in one of the country's newest and fastest pools. Walking into the enormous building, I gaped at the impossibly high ceiling and marveled at the sleek gutter system that allowed water to flow over the edge of the pool onto the deck without creating waves along the walls. I encountered several big names in the warm-up pool, like world record holder Mary T. Meagher and American record holders Tracey Caulkins and Sue Walsh. At those nationals, I did my best to compete and not compare. Many of the athletes were older or taller than me. Many had swum faster times than me in previous meets and motored past me in the warm-up pool. I put my face in the water and blocked out everything and everyone to remain intently focused on my races.

I swam well in the preliminary heats of the 100-meter backstroke and qualified for the finals. That evening, I was nervous but calm while my teammates cheered and gave me high fives as I paraded onto the deck with the seven other finalists. I felt the support and encouragement from my team and knew I would swim fast. It was thrilling to race against a talented field and finish in second place. Sue Walsh, the reigning American record holder in the event, finished first. Several days later, I placed 10th in the 200-meter backstroke.

Two years later, at the 1984 Olympic Trials in Indianapolis, I relied on the same game plan. The United States Olympic Swimming Trials is one of the most stressful events on the planet. In most races, only the top two finishers make the team. There are exceptions in the 100 and 200 freestyle races because they need to field a team of four swimmers for the relay events. But in the 100 backstroke, I had to place first or second to qualify for the Olympic team. I had heard people say that making the U.S. Olympic team in swimming was more difficult than reaching the finals at the Olympic Games because the depth of swimming talent in the United States is staggering. I knew there were swimmers I needed to beat, but I refused to worship past winners or record-holders or even think about the person in the lane next to me. By ignoring the people in the stands who cheered for my competitors, I avoided thinking about what came after the race. I focused entirely on what I was doing at that moment. It was the essence of being present and the definition of total focus. After a terrific morning swim, I qualified first in the preliminary heats of the 100 backstroke.

During the afternoon before the finals of my race, I sat on the carpet in the hallway outside my hotel room. While my roommates relaxed inside the room on the beds, laughing and entertaining their friends, I wanted to be alone. I was a jumble of emotions and wrote in my journal that I wished I were talking like all the other girls, but

I didn't know what to say. My brain felt scrambled, and my mood shifted erratically from nervous to excited, and from anxious to confident. Everyone at the Olympic Trials wanted the same thing, to make the team, but only two in each event would succeed. Writing in my journal seemed to calm me down: *"I feel confident and sure that regardless of the outcome, I will have learned a lot and had fun."* Looking back, it's great to know I had a positive attitude: *"People are worried and worrying. They're trying to impress everyone else by socializing and pretending to keep cool."* I remained in the hall because I didn't want to deal with the nerves and stress of others. The challenge for me to stay focused on my race and keep my emotions in check was enough. It wasn't just the athletes who were nervous. I wrote about my coach: *"He needs to relax and stop thinking so much. So do I. I'm ready. I just know my body wants to go and my mind has to let it do its thing."*

My grandmothers, my parents, brother, and several friends from Marietta, Ohio traveled to Indianapolis to watch the Olympic Trials. Unfortunately, I had to block them out of my mind. When it was time for me to race, the eight finalists paraded onto the pool deck to our starting positions. I felt pumped as Van Halen's "Right Now" played on my Sony Walkman. Striding past my Cincinnati teammates in the bleachers, I remember them screaming for me, and I glanced at my best friend, Betsy. "You got this!" she yelled, pumping her fist, as I turned the corner and took my place behind lane four. When an official blew the whistle, I jumped into the pool for the start of the race. [7] As I gripped the starting block with my hands and positioned my feet on the wall, I heard the "all quiet" whistle from the official. My brother shouted one final cheer, "Go Betsy!" My heart pounded like a drum inside my chest as I curled upwards like a spring, ready to release backwards. When the starting pistol sounded, I exploded from the blocks, stretching and streamlining my body, kicking myself to the surface.

---

7 Backstroke races start in the water, and swimmers must enter the pool in their specific lane before the race begins..

I don't remember the first half of the race, but I peeked at the gigantic scoreboard as I turned at the 50-meter mark; I was in fourth place. Apparently, up in the stands, my dad was too nervous to watch the race, so he left the arena and walked out into the hallway. He later told me he couldn't handle the stress, to have me work so hard and get that far, and not make the team. I laughed later when we spoke about this because I had promised myself I would leave nothing in the pool that day. My confidence and performance in the second half of my races have always been strong. I relished finishing fast, pumping my arms, kicking my legs, churning through the water all the way to the wall. At those 1984 Olympic Trials, I did exactly what my mom always told me to do long ago when she taught me how to swim. Kick! Kick! Kick! When I touched the wall at the end of the race, I wasn't immediately aware of how I had finished because of my poor eyesight. I squinted and stared at the scoreboard as my Cincinnati teammates whistled and cheered. A photographer caught my reaction after I saw the number "one" next to my name. The photos showed my pure joy, exhilaration, and triumph. I had bested a field of Olympians, national champions, and friends. I felt shocked, elated, and fired-up to qualify for my first Olympics.

The next steps in my life were a blur. After the Trials, the team assembled immediately and flew to California. There was no chance to go home, so I said goodbye to my parents, my coach, and my friends. Thankfully, two other members of the Cincinnati team qualified for the Olympics. One of them was my backstroke training partner, Dave Wilson, so I didn't feel completely alone. Only a few pre-selected coaches led the Olympic team, so I had to adapt to training with a new leader. We stayed in a hotel in Mission Viejo for a few weeks before the Games and trained at the Nadadores' pool. Like me, many of the athletes didn't have their coach working with them to prepare for their races, and to me, it seemed like all my U.S. teammates trained longer and harder in the pool. I remember telling myself to trust my gut. My gut had gotten me there. I knew what I needed to do, and part of that was taking care of myself and doing what was right for me. When the coach told me to swim a particular set or hold a specific pace, if that didn't seem right for me, I didn't ignore the command, but I swam through it. I went through the motions and focused on the training habits that had gotten me to the Olympics. It wasn't ideal, but in those moments, I had to rely on my instincts and not compare myself to others who were accustomed to a different training style. That lesson became a strength of mine, and I learned to stay within myself and do what felt right for me.

Two years later, I learned not to place limits on myself based on someone else's best performance. At the U.S. Swimming World Championship Trials in Orlando, Florida, during the summer of 1986, I qualified first in the preliminary heats of the 200-meter backstroke, setting an American record in the event. Competing for Longhorn Aquatics and alongside many of my Texas teammates, I had lowered my best time by two seconds during that morning race. My coach, Richard Quick, asked me about the race, "Was it hard? You were supposed to hold back." The race had felt like practice when I held a pace of 32 seconds for multiple 50-meter repetitions. Richard nodded and told me to get some lunch and rest before the finals. I don't remember getting much rest, but the team ate at Wendy's almost every day during that meet, and I ordered my usual single with cheese, onion, tomato, and lettuce with fries.

That evening, after a brief team meeting to review the night's events, we loaded into vans and drove to the Justice Aquatic Center. Music blared from the car speakers, and I chatted with my teammates to pass the time. I stretched before my race and swam the bulk of my warm-up in a secondary pool to avoid the crowds in the competition pool. When I felt calm and loose, I found Richard on the pool deck for pace work. I nailed my 32 second per length pace and didn't bother to practice any starts.

In the ready room before the 200 backstroke final, I greeted friends but didn't socialize. I donned headphones and listened to Bruce Springsteen before I cranked my favorite Van Halen fire-up song. Later, as we paraded onto the deck, I calmed the bat wings in my stomach and tried not to think. Behind lane four, after the announcer had called my name and I waved to the crowd, I dipped my goggles into the water and removed my sweatsuit. When the official blew the whistle, I dove into the pool to prepare for the start. As the next whistle sounded, I gripped the starting block with my hands and set my feet high on the wall. The starter asked for quiet and reminded the competitors that the race was four lengths of the pool backstroke. My mind went blank as I crouched and waited for the starter's signal.

When I heard the BLEEP, I exploded off the wall, flinging my arms behind my head, kicking to the surface. The first length of the pool felt easy as I kept my arm and leg tempo steady. I attacked the first turn and leaped off the wall, kicking and staying under the water to avoid turbulence. The next two lengths were a blur because I felt amazing: smooth, floaty, like I was swimming on a cloud. When I turned at the 150-meter mark, I was ahead in the race and could hear the roar of the crowd. With one length to go, the noise in the aquatic center propelled me to maintain my arm and leg speed, even though I thought my lungs might burst. When I reached the final flags with five meters to go, I almost blacked out, but touched the wall with my hand and whipped off my goggles. Some of my competitors hadn't finished the race yet, but the stands erupted with screams and whistles as the announcer shouted, "NEW WORLD RECORD!"

As I let the words sink in and saw my time of 2:08.60, I pumped my fist and searched the crowd for my parents. I had bested a time swum by Cornelia Sirch, an athlete who later admitted to doping as part of the East German training system. Although I hadn't expected to go that fast, I had trained for and swum a nearly perfect race. At that meet, Pablo Morales, Matt Biondi, and I each set world records, and we later graced the cover of *Swimming World Magazine*. The writers called it the re-emergence of American swimming.

My 200-meter backstroke record, set on June 27, 1986, stood for five years until August 25, 1991. In that year, the backstroke turn rules changed and swimmers no longer needed to touch the wall with their hand. The new rule allowed backstrokers, as they approached the wall, to take one stroke across their body and rotate onto their stomach for a flip turn where only a swimmer's feet touch the wall. Krisztina Egerszegi, a talented Hungarian swimmer, used the newer, faster flip turn during her race at the European Championships to break my record. After the rule change, swimmers all over the world set new backstroke records in almost every pool, team, and competition. While Egerszegi broke my 200-meter backstroke world record soon after the rule change, my time, which was also an American record, stood for sixteen years. [8]

Several years later, when I took up rowing the double scull, I again ignored the comments and expectations of others. Because I was a beginner in the sport, established rowers expected me and my partner Cecile to race poorly, even though Cecile was a veteran Harvard rower. But the sport of rowing shares many similarities with swimming. You must break the surface of the water and place your oar (or hand in swimming), then move the boat (or your body) past that point. Both rowers and swimmers must glide and maximize their distance per stroke. Athletes in these two sports rely on high lung capacity, strong legs, and finding a steady rhythm. During a race, rowers and swimmers rely on pacing and rowers often divide longer distances into shorter increments, like the lengths of a pool. Some major differences are temperature and wind. Swimming meets typically occur indoors, while rowing events take place outdoors. And unless you row as a single, working with a partner, quad, or boat of eight oarsmen, can be tricky. I also found rowing more difficult physically because I raced for six to seven minutes, rather than one or two minutes.

In 1993, Cecile and I had some success and qualified for a regatta in Lucerne, Switzerland. I enjoyed traveling for a new sport, meeting other rowers and visiting other countries. One year later,

---

8 On August 15, 2002, Natalie Coughlin set an American record in the 200-meter backstroke with a time of 2:08.53.

we raced in Princeton, New Jersey at the 1994 U.S. trials for the Rowing World Championships. After loads of practice, we blocked out the chatter and focused on our race, the 2,000-meter distance. We showed up to compete, not compare. Cecile and I finished first in the event and qualified for the World Championships. Although we felt confident in our ability to race, our performance shocked almost everyone else in attendance.

As a young woman, I experienced some incredible moments in sports. By not concerning myself with what others had done and instead focusing on my training and races, I made myself proud, even when I didn't finish first. Of course, I wasn't perfect, and like many teen and pre-teen girls, I sometimes struggled with body image. As a girl, I wanted to be feminine, but I've always had broad shoulders and narrow hips. At some point, I realized I would never have a womanly hourglass figure. And like many young girls, I felt conflicted about being attractive and was afraid my muscles would turn people off. It took some time, but I eventually realized that a serious athlete must develop traditionally masculine traits like aggressiveness and assertiveness. You need muscles for strength and stamina. Training is hard, sweaty work, and to improve, you must push your body to perform. Rather than worry about my physique, I learned to embrace the beauty of a perfectly executed flip turn, the rhythmic undulation of a butterfly stroke, and found satisfaction in being physically fit.

I have always been competitive, but as I grew older, I developed a self-centered mentality regarding sports. My goal in training wasn't to defeat others or race to make an impression; I raced for myself. There was a lot of satisfaction involved. Winning was nice, but not essential. My favorite quote from an unknown source guided me, and I kept the words in my locker and on my desk: "If the records and the first-place trophy come, fine. But I get in the water to swim." It's a challenge to keep improving your times or your game. The reality is you will not record a personal best every time you compete, but if you love swimming or your sport enough, you don't dwell on that. You get fired up for the next race and the chance to improve.

For parents and coaches, please know there is no benefit to comparisons. Telling your child another player is faster, stronger, or better, doesn't help. Most likely, the child already knows this. For a parent to be helpful, they must focus on the child and their individual development and progress. For coaches, telling your players the other team is making 80% of their shots will not help your team score more points. Reminding the team they are losing doesn't help either. A coach must find positive ways to instruct or encourage the players and not focus on the opponent.

Every day at the California Institute of Technology (Caltech), where I work as the director of athletics, I face this situation. As a Division III school, it serves zero purpose to compare our sports programs with nearby Division I schools like the University of Southern California and the University of California, Los Angeles. It's also unnecessary to compare our athletic teams with local Division III schools like Occidental College or Pomona College. At Caltech, our teams focus on their own progress, making incremental improvement, raising self-confidence, and developing school pride.

No sport at Caltech exemplifies this more than our baseball team. When I joined the university in 2011, the team hadn't won many games. During my tenure, the baseball team ended a 10-year, 228 game winless streak in non-conference games, and a 29-year, over 600 game, winless streak in conference games. I remember speaking with prospective students, asking them if they wanted to play baseball for Caltech. The ones who loved the sport agreed and made a commitment to work hard and improve their game. It took two years of intense focus, training, and believing in themselves for the baseball team to win a non-conference game. [9] It took the team four more years, until 2017, to snap the conference losing

---

9 On February 2, 2013, the Caltech Beavers won 9-7 over Pacifica College.

streak. [10] The players' and coaches' dedication produced incremental improvement, and they finally achieved their goal. Two years later, the team earned 10 wins during a single season. Rather than comparing themselves to other schools and coming up short, the Caltech baseball team made a commitment to compete and strive to be their best on the field during every practice and game.

I tell athletes everywhere of all ages and in all sports, "Dare to be your best." Work hard and have fun, but remember to avoid comparing yourself to anyone else. Comparing leads to thoughts like, "They're better than me," or "I'm not good enough." It takes the focus off yourself and your personal goals. Comparing also leads to "winner" and "loser" labels, which are unnecessary and destructive. Ignore those thoughts and accept where you are. Play the game and have fun while thinking about how you can improve. And if you must compare, compare yourself to your own past performances. Only you know if you have put in the work to be competitive or if you prefer recreational play. Either way, sports are supposed to be fun, not a journey of mental pain and angst.

---

10 On March 31, 2017, in the Southern California Intercollegiate Athletic Conference, Caltech won 4-3 over Pomona Pitzer Colleges.

Before the 200-meter backstroke race at world championship trials in 1986.

Receiving a gold medal at the world championship trials after swimming a world record time of 2:08.60 in the 200-meter backstroke.

All smiles during the gold medal ceremony for the 100-meter backstroke at the 1986 World Championships in Madrid, Spain.

Age 26 competing at the Head of
the Charles Regatta in a single scull.

Age 28 training with Cecile (me on
the left) on the Charles River.

CHAPTER
5

BENEFIT FROM BROAD EXPERIENCE

I want to make the case for broad athletic experience, especially for children. There is a risk in forcing a child to specialize too soon. For most kids, it's not sustainable or causes emotional distress. Enjoying a variety of activities makes life more fun and prevents burn-out. Plus, it prioritizes opportunities to learn diverse skills. The hand-eye coordination needed for ball sports like baseball, volleyball, and basketball can transfer to tennis or golf. The fitness gained from playing soccer benefits football and lacrosse players, as well as runners. Athletes gain physiological benefits by using different muscle groups during exercise. They experience a cross-training effect, and I believe young people can extend their development by avoiding overspecialization.

Specializing in one sport too soon can also lead to injury. Overuse injuries, especially to shoulders, are common in baseball and softball pitchers, as well as in swimmers and volleyball players. Knee pain is common in soccer and volleyball players, as well as runners. For many years, I avoided these types of injuries by not focusing entirely on swimming when I was young. I also trained moderately throughout most of my teens and took regular time off from practice and competition.

Focusing on a single sport at an early age may also prevent a child from finding their true talent in another arena. It's not uncommon for young gymnasts who lack a passion for the sport to try trampoline, cheer, springboard diving, or even pole-vaulting. Likewise, a young swimmer may prefer water polo or triathlon. Kids who start out playing soccer often choose track and field, lacrosse, or basketball in their teens. For most children growing up in the United States, it's better to try every sport of interest while the time commitment and expense are minimal. This gives kids time to learn a variety of skills and find an activity that drives their internal motivation.

Many of today's top athletes competed in multiple sports growing up, and that seems like the best strategy for most children. If a kid loves sports, encourage them to try several to help them develop as an all-around athlete. Football players often play basketball or participate in track and field. Basketball players frequently play volleyball, and many swimmers play water polo. Tom Brady, LeBron James, and Megan Rapinoe are three examples of professional athletes who developed slowly through middle school and high school. Tom Brady played football, baseball, and basketball; LeBron James played basketball, football, and ran track; and Megan Rapinoe played soccer but also ran track and played basketball. Each of them played multiple sports before their focus solidified in college or as a professional player. I am convinced their participation in several sports contributed to longevity in their professional careers. Of course, there are exceptions like gymnast Simone Biles and swimmer Michael Phelps, who focused solely on one sport, but considering the millions of kids playing sports, I believe broad experience is the better teacher.

Unfortunately, focusing on one sport year-round has become commonplace, even for children under age 10. Coaches often mandate a full-time commitment to a single sport. I don't believe these restrictions benefit kids, but I'm guessing they benefit the coaches who lead the club and travel teams. Families end up paying hundreds of dollars or more each month to keep their children in youth sports. I understand that many parents hope their child will earn a college scholarship or play professionally, but most never will. It seems more logical for parents to invest their family's resources in education rather than in their child's sport. In my experience, expecting a future in sports is not a good bet.

Although I may sound a bit hypocritical because I spent most of my youth in the pool swimming, I have a diverse background in sports. I learned to play tennis and took ballet classes as a child. Because of the heavy racket and the strain on my arm from hitting the ball, tennis wasn't a sport I enjoyed. I tolerated ballet for a brief time, but found it too regimented and boring. In grade school, I preferred swimming or running around outside with my brother and his friends. In middle school, I ran track and played volleyball. I remember volleyball hurt my arms, and I didn't like being hit with the ball. I also recall having to run the 800-meters in a track meet and found it incredibly painful. Neither of those sports grabbed my attention or made me smile, but I tried them. I also took part in a bunch of activities during my time at summer camp. From age eight to 14, I attended camp and learned canoeing, judo, water-skiing, sailing, rifle-shooting, archery, and horseback riding. I truly enjoyed trying these new sports, especially anything on the water, and I looked forward to attending camp for this reason.

In high school at the Mercersburg Academy in Pennsylvania, our swimming coach encouraged us to play water polo when the swimming season had ended. We had a brief season with only a few games, but I benefited from the change in training. Playing water polo took the focus off racing and the pace clock and placed it on team strategy. I also threw the shot put at several high school track meets simply because my strength allowed me to throw farther than the other girls at my school. This diversity of experience and activity not only made me realize my genuine passion was swimming, but also helped prevent overuse injuries and burnout.

Today, most young swimmers incorporate some type of cross-training into their schedules and every sport has strength and conditioning building blocks. The most common activities are weightlifting, stretching, and running for overall fitness. My exposure to cross-training began at the Parkersburg YMCA with a Universal Gym that had stations for bench press, Lat pull, biceps, and triceps. Twice each week before swimming practice, we used the five or six stations to improve our strength. When I enrolled at the Mercersburg Academy as a high school junior, our coach introduced me to a different type of dry land training. My teammates and I completed a circuit of exercises meant to mimic the motion of swimming and increase stamina. It was hard work that made my muscles ache for days after each session, but when we reduced the dry land training near the end of the season, I noticed an increase in my strength and power in the pool. I exploded off the blocks at the start of a race and leaped off the walls after each flip turn.

As a freshman in college at the University of North Carolina, our swim team performed Jane Fonda-style aerobics to enhance our fitness. Jane Fonda, an award-winning actress, was famous for combining calisthenics and music with a movie star vibe. Several times per week before swim practice, we followed the commands of an instructor and stepped, kicked, and jumped to the music. This type of exercise was some of the hardest I had ever endured.

Later, at the University of Texas at Austin (UT), our team ran several times per week for an hour and lifted weights regularly, keeping a chart of our exercises and repetitions. The atmosphere in the weight room at UT was intense and competitive. I believe it was the first time I worked systematically to break down my muscles so they could build back stronger. Our coach also required us to do pull-ups or chin-ups. Some of my teammates, like Jodi and Colleen, had very high strength-to-weight ratios and could easily (or they made it look easy) perform twenty pull-ups in a row; I was not one of those people. As hard as I tried to pull myself up and raise my chin over the bar, I needed my weight-training partner to give me a boost to complete the set. I eventually performed an unassisted pull-up when I started rowing at age 25 in 1991. Several years later, I could do 15 without help.

I also reaped the benefit of trying many sports at a young age when I arrived at UT. The women's athletic director, Dr. Donna Lopiano, had been a stellar softball player. During our fall orientation in 1984, she arranged a friendly game for the new female athletes. My brother and I had played baseball, so I was familiar with the game, but there were several freshman swimmers on our team who had never held a baseball bat or worn a glove. They had to be taught how to follow the ball with their eyes, swing a bat, and use a glove to field a ground ball. With my exposure to baseball, tennis, and volleyball as a young girl, I didn't feel like a fish out of water and enjoyed playing in the softball game. Other athletes, whether swimmers, golfers, or runners, struggled with the new activity.

As an undergraduate student at UT, I majored in education with a focus on coaching. I took a class called Introduction to Racquet Sports. For that course, I learned several new sports and, for the final exam, had to teach the skills and rules associated with squash, tennis, and racquetball. My early exposure to a variety of sports was invaluable. I caught on quickly and became especially fond of squash, which I played for many years and still enjoy today.

When my swimming days ended, my experience with cross-training also helped me transition to competitive rowing in my 20s. My overall fitness has allowed me to take active vacations where hiking and cycling are a focal point of my travels. As I continue to age, regular strength training and stretching provide a solid foundation for a healthy life. I also play golf, ride my mountain bike, and enjoy stand-up paddling. Having a history in various sports has smoothed the way when I try something new. Within the last few years, I have added pickleball to my repertoire. My previous experience with tennis, ping-pong, and squash helped me to learn pickleball quickly and seamlessly feel confident with the new sport.

Most people, myself included, only play sports for fun. We enjoy the process of training and challenging ourselves to improve. I also enjoy the social aspects of sports, especially pickleball and golf. Players have time to chat during these games and compete for bragging rights. Winning has little value in these recreational endeavors and I stay active because it's part of my daily routine. Sports benefit my physical and mental health, and by having a variety of experiences both in and out of the water, I have been able to pivot and try new activities with less strain or risk of injury.

When I meet someone new and they learn about my swimming history, their first question for me is always, "Do you still swim?" I usually chuckle and shake my head. I rarely swim anymore, but it's not because I'm avoiding the sport. Swimming never felt like a job to me, even when I was training every day. But swimming is a solitary activity, and as I age, I gravitate towards more dynamic sports that I can enjoy with others. Besides the social aspect of playing sports, I crave the outdoors, fresh air, and new challenges. As an adventurous person, I want to learn new things, and these days, there are just so many other activities to try.

For amateur sports coaches, don't punish a player for participating in multiple sports. Instead, work with the athlete to help them achieve their goals and learn new skills. By playing sports, kids are learning far more about themselves, how to work together, and what they enjoy doing. These are life lessons that last longer than a fleeting victory or a state title. Allowing kids to discover a variety of activities at a young age sets the stage for a more active and healthy life in the future.

While working as athletic director at the Laurel School, Allegheny College, and Caltech, I've helped athletes and coaches accommodate multi-sport athletes. I don't see the need for a motivated player to choose between two sports they love. At Laurel, I worked with a high school soccer player who also wanted to play basketball. Once the young athlete took the lead and made a commitment to her schoolwork and sports, I worked with the coaches to devise a transition from one sport to the other. At Allegheny, I assisted a field hockey player who also played lacrosse. It took a bit of compromise for the coaches, but they understood the athlete's choice to excel at both. It was a personal decision for the athlete, not a lack of commitment to the team or a show of disrespect for the coach. If the athlete, coaches, and athletic departments work together, it is possible for students to play more than one sport in high school and college.

I sometimes wonder if my swimming career would've been different had I focused solely on swimming during my youth. I'll never know, but I believe a broad and varied athletic experience offers the most benefits for children. Enjoying a variety of activities didn't hold me back, and I encourage parents to set guidelines for their children in this department. Just because a coach holds practice year-round doesn't mean your child has to play without a break. And for parents who see talent in their child and have a fantasy in their minds that they're raising a future professional athlete, stepping back and giving your child time to blossom and develop their own passion is crucial. I understand the power of watching your kid dominate in a game or crush the competition. It feels great, but a parent's bragging rights, or ego boost, should not trump proper development of their child. By specializing too soon, a young athlete risks injury, burn-out, or regret in not finding their passion. Diversity of activity sets the stage for a more active, happy, and healthy life.

Age 4
experimenting
with the guitar.

Age 7 before a
Brownie troop meeting
at my house.

Age 6 practicing
my ballet pose.

Age 7 riding a horse at Camp Tippecanoe.

Age 9 getting ready to play tennis.

Age 7 on cross country skis in the front yard of my house.

CHAPTER
6

WORK TOWARDS GOALS

Every athlete has big dreams. What basketball player doesn't want to sink the buzzer-beating shot? What football player doesn't want to catch the winning touchdown? It's fun to imagine yourself winning a national championship or being an Olympian. Dreams are wonderful and have a place in our minds, but the omni-present images on television fuel a fantasy for athletes that is disconnected from reality. Setting goals and working towards them are more important. Having short-term goals about milestones a person can control is the most helpful, especially for young athletes.

What can a person control? One answer is not whether they win a game or a race. An athlete can do everything right and perform their best, but still lose. Athletes can only control their effort, attitude, and dedication, and many athletic programs now train their students in this. By setting goals based on these principles, young athletes can make incremental progress towards a goal, and that progress sustains and boosts their motivation by providing the stepping stones for success.

Regular attendance at practice for any sport or avocation shows dedication to a goal. Without steady practice, it's nearly impossible to improve performance. By making attendance a goal, children take the first step towards improvement. As a parent, if your child doesn't want to attend practice, find out why; don't just force them to go. They may not like the coach or their teammates. If that's the case, at an appropriate point, try a different team. If a child doesn't like the game or the sport, it's probably time to find another activity for them. And parents, this isn't about you. This is an opportunity for your child to decide what they like and what they want to do.

During practice or training, an athlete must give effort and be self-driven to improve. If a child finds an activity fun and feels motivated to get better, working hard will come naturally. For other kids, those who ignore the coach, disobey instructions, or routinely skip the drills, it's clear they're not interested in that sport, and that's fine. Once a parent acknowledges their child isn't trying during practice or is disrupting others, it's best to attempt something new. There is a fine line, however, between supporting a child's learning and effort and forcing compliance. If possible, complete the class session or sports season, then find another activity that captures the child's attention.

The entire process begins with a positive attitude. Staying positive helps an athlete handle the inevitable mistakes and losses, as well as the unexpected wins. Parents and coaches also play a critical role in this arena. It's more important to look ahead to the next opportunity than to dwell on past mistakes. None of us can change what has already happened, so the clearest path is forward. Athletes, coaches, and parents need to remind themselves that it's just one workout or one game. Yes, it might be a monumental moment like the Olympic Games or a national championship game, but it's still one moment. Viewing the loss or mistake through this lens allows one to reflect, learn, and focus on the future. As a young swimmer, I never consciously thought about any of these things. I loved swimming and simply wanted to go to practice, work hard, and get faster.

When I watched the 1976 Olympics as a child, I don't recall viewing any swimming races, but a few of the other sports sparked my interest. I recall the incredible performances by Bruce Jenner in decathlon and Nadia Comaneci in gymnastics. There was something about the Games that captured my imagination. It may have been the beaming faces of the winning competitors or the exquisite performances from the athletes, but I felt smitten. In 1978, my 12-year-old self typed a note and taped it to the outside of my bedroom door. I informed my mom I was going to morning workout and needed to bring a lunch. I also mentioned an upcoming science project and an English report that needed work. The note ended with: *"That's about it for tonight. From ABC news, this is Howard Cosell signing off from the 1984 Olympics where Betsy Mitchell has just received the gold medal in the 100 free."*

I dreamed of being an Olympian, but it wasn't truly a goal at age 12. As a young athlete, it was a fantasy. Tom Phillips, my coach at the Parkersburg YMCA, introduced me to more specific goal-setting that year. The most common goals in swimming are time-based. For instance, you may want to break one minute for a particular race or swim a specific qualifying time standard (such as an Olympic Trials qualifying time). Another more ambiguous goal is to swim a personal best time in a race. Track and field goals are similar, but other sports do not evaluate performance based on time. Diving, gymnastics, and figure skating all rely upon difficulty and scoring; the latter has a factor of subjectivity. To earn higher scores in a competition, an athlete may set a goal to increase their level of difficulty. Other individual sports like tennis or golf allow for flexibility in goals, like missing fewer serves in tennis or making more pars in golf. Team sports offer fewer opportunities for individual goals, as most are team-related but individual elements may arise. In football, each player may work towards a penalty-free game. In basketball, a player's goal might be to avoid being called for a foul or to make 90 percent of their free-throw shots. Whatever the goal, if it's specific and personal, you are more likely to focus on achieving it.

This doesn't mean a parent or coach tells an athlete their goals. Whether for an individual or a team, goals must be self-directed. A coach or parent may guide, but not interfere as a young athlete develops a personal plan. A baseball player who sets a goal to have more hits may need help from their coach or parents to practice batting. If the player hits more balls during practice and at the batting cages, they're likely to connect with the ball more frequently in a game. By practicing what they want to achieve, a child takes a step towards improvement. It works the same in basketball with free throws. Few teams actually practice free throw shooting during team training, so it's up to the athlete to find time to practice that particular shot. Through dedication and repetition, a player proves to themselves they can do it. Coach Tom didn't tell me my goals. Instead, he asked me about them, and it was my responsibility to own them and dream them. At age 11, my goal was simple: in each race, to swim faster than I had before.

In swimming, it's easy to connect training to racing. A swimmer trains at a certain pace, so they're confident they can swim at that pace during a race. Coaches are a big help. By making it a goal to train at a particular pace, a swimmer becomes more confident on race day. I encourage young athletes in any sport to come up with their own goals, or have the team generate a list of goals for a game or the season, or both. Although "winning every game" is a tempting goal, athletes don't have control over that. Other options are more manageable, like scoring at least one goal in every soccer game or preventing a quarterback sack in football.

There are many ways to set goals. An athlete can work alone, with their coach or parent, or keep a journal. Written goals are often more effective than unwritten goals. I started tracking my training in notebooks during my early teens, writing the daily workout and commenting on its difficulty. If the sets were challenging, I would put a star next to them and record some of my practice times. In the future, if we repeated the set, I compared my progress to track my improvement. I wasn't always meticulous and sometimes my journal simply said, "Practice was hard," "My body hurts," or "I was slow today." I also kept a tally of the specific times I swam in each event at meets. Over the years, when I looked back at my progress, my improvement became clear.

Another benefit of setting goals is to keep the focus on your own training and performance, which is all you can control. An athlete driven by goals takes charge of the process, minimizing distractions about what others are doing. This is incredibly important because it is impossible to control others, whether they're on your team or they're your opponent. The ability for a team to win is not within the control of an individual, so it's dangerous and usually unattainable to make winning a goal. I speak from experience when I say you can swim a personal best time and not win. When that happens, don't despair. Even if you don't medal, it's satisfying to perform your best. You achieved a goal. You can also encourage and support a teammates' journey, knowing you can only control your own attitude and thoughts, your own effort and actions.

In 1982, as a high school junior, I set a national high school record in the 100-yard backstroke with a time of 58.30 seconds at the Eastern Interscholastic Swimming and Diving Championships. My goal for that meet was to swim my best times and contribute to a Mercersburg team victory. I didn't focus on a particular number or record time. Back at school after the meet, when I met with Coach JT for a goal-setting talk, he sat me down in his office and told me I was going to be an Olympian. I had laughed at him, but he was serious. "What are your summer plans?" he asked. I had planned to return home to Marietta and swim with the Parkersburg YMCA team, but JT had planted a seed in my brain; I could do more. Our conversation made me ponder my goals, and after the words had sunk in, I reviewed my progress in the pool. I realized I had talent and if I worked harder, the possibilities were endless. It was the first time that my dream of going to the Olympics became a goal.

At that moment, it seemed possible to make the Olympic team, but I needed to be faster. Swimming with a different coach and a better team seemed like a logical step towards my goal.

When my school year at Mercersburg ended, I moved to Cincinnati, Ohio, for the summer to train with the Pepsi Marlins, a big commercial swimming club that operated with a business model. Hundreds of athletes swam on the team. They divided the swimmers into beginners, intermediates, and elite national-caliber athletes. Coach Jay Fitzgerald welcomed me to the national group based on my times, but immediately assigned me to lane one, the gutter lane. I understood his reasoning. I had trained infrequently in a 50-meter pool. Most of my previous training had been in 25-yard pools, which provide more opportunities to rest for a split-second during flip turns. Despite my lane assignment, I believe it helped me in the long run. During training, multiple swimmers occupy a lane and "circle" in a counterclockwise direction (in Europe they often swim clockwise), keeping the lane line on their right. Swimming next to the wall, every other length, forced me to rotate my hips and shoulders during backstroke sets so my hand didn't scrape the wall. I also couldn't pull on the lane line as frequently as those in the center lanes of the pool. In a subtle way, these factors allowed me to become stronger and more efficient in the water.

That summer in 1982, I earned an invitation to the National Sports Festival in Indianapolis, Indiana. Held during the summer, Sports Fest is an annual multi-sport competition where athletes are divided into teams by region. I was on the North team and met many swimmers from around the country. The meet was another chance for me to compete against some of the best swimmers in the United States. My training in Cincinnati also prepared me for my breakout performance that same summer at the national championships when I finished second in the 100-meter backstroke.

Another technique that helped me achieve my goals was visualization. I learned this from an assistant coach in Cincinnati.

Visualization means envisioning a particular activity or race in your mind without physically performing the activity. Every night before going to sleep, I would lie on my back and close my eyes. In my mind, I saw myself swimming the 100-meter backstroke from start to finish like it was race day. In my head, I felt my arm tempo and leg drive. I visualized my arms churning like a steady windmill, my legs kicking and boiling the water, and my body hydroplaning above the water. I would use a stopwatch and time my visualization. As my technique improved, it would take me about one minute to "swim" the race, which was very close to the times I swam the actual event in the pool. My intent was to make the race familiar, so I would be confident before an actual race, knowing I had swum the event hundreds of times. I also found it to be a great way to calm my nerves. Visualization became an integral part of my goal setting to make the 1984 Olympic team, and it also had a tremendous impact on the rest of my life. For about two decades after I stopped swimming, I could not fall asleep unless I was lying on my back, like when I had been visualizing myself swimming.

In 1984, after the NCAA swimming championships in March, I knew I needed to leave the University of North Carolina (UNC) team and train with Coach Jay in Cincinnati if I wanted to achieve my Olympic goal. Under Jay's guidance the previous summers, I had made tremendous progress, and I knew that every member of his elite team remained focused on the Olympic Trials in June. I had felt the urge to leave UNC sooner but waited until after the NCAA meet. My dad's advice, *to evaluate at the end, not in the middle*, guided my plans. I waited for the collegiate season to conclude and immediately moved to Cincinnati to train for the Olympic Trials.

After reaching my goal of making the Olympic team, I struggled to set a realistic goal for the Olympic Games that didn't focus on winning. I wanted to swim a best time, possibly break one minute in the 100-meter backstroke, but I also wanted to race well. Unfortunately, I failed to meet my goals, and that happens sometimes. It was disappointing but not disastrous. After those

Olympics, I immediately refocused my attitude, dedication, and effort when I transferred to the University of Texas at Austin (UT). I had to sit out for one year of eligibility, which is called "redshirting," because I had swum for UNC the previous year. During my redshirt year, I trained with the Texas team but couldn't compete for the university, so my goals shifted to traveling, racing abroad, and having fun. Because I had been an Olympian, I was a member of the U.S. National Team, and I competed in swimming meets in Perth, Australia, Bonn, Germany, and Monte Carlo, Monaco. I felt incredibly lucky to travel the world competing for Team USA.

As a college junior at UT, at the suggestion of my coach, Richard Quick, I experimented with an unorthodox method of goal setting. It began with an empty glass jar and a bag of colored marbles. The marbles sitting in a bag next to the jar were a way for me to stay focused on my goals. I was at a stage where improvements in my times were difficult to achieve. My times were already fast, so I felt like I needed a different tactic to improve, even by a fraction of a second. I felt motivated to fill the jar with marbles to connect my behavior outside of the pool with my performance in the pool. At the end of each day, I evaluated my behavior. I added a marble to the jar if I went for a run after swimming practice. Another marble went into the jar when I went to bed early or achieved a personal best in the weight room. I removed a marble if I drank alcohol or soda, or if I indulged in ice cream. At the suggestion of the team trainer, I also gave up bologna sandwiches, which were my favorite. It may sound rigid or obsessive, but at the end of the season at the NCAA championship meet, I wanted to look at the jar filled with marbles and know I had done everything I could to get better.

At those championships in 1987, I had one of the best meets of my life. Texas earned its fourth straight team title, and I won three individual events and contributed to several relay wins. Besides winning both the 100- and 200-yard backstroke, I also won the 200-yard individual medley (IM). The 200-yard IM is a race that requires an athlete to swim 50 yards each of butterfly, backstroke, breaststroke, and freestyle, in that order. The event requires speed and proficiency in each stroke. I cherished that win because no one except my coach and I expected me to perform that well. I was the top scorer of the meet and MVP of my Texas team. Later that year, I received the Honda-Broderick Sport Cup, an award given annually to the top female collegiate athletes.

Despite my success, I never achieved one of my top goals: to break one minute in the 100-meter backstroke. I had written the number 59.6 on my pull buoy and on a poster I kept in my swimming locker. It was a constant reminder of my goal. When I retired from swimming after the 1988 Olympics, my body needed a break from training, but I never lost sight of that specific goal. One year later, I returned to the pool for a last effort to achieve my goal of breaking one minute. Swimming well in 1990, I qualified for the inaugural Goodwill Games, an international sporting event created by Ted Turner after the 1980 and 1984 political boycotts of the Olympics by many nations. [11] In Seattle, Washington, at the Goodwill Games, I finished first in the 100-meter backstroke with a time of 1:01.46. I had swum faster in the preliminary heats, equaling my personal best and American record time of 1:01.20, but my goal eluded me. I imagine if I had stuck with the sport longer, one more year, when they changed the backstroke flip turn rules (allowing a swimmer to flip without touching the wall with their hand), I might have achieved my goal. Backstroke times improved dramatically after that rule change in 1991, but when I retired for the second time, for good, I didn't know the flip turn rules would soon change. After giving it my all and not achieving my goal in 1990, I knew it was time to move on. New challenges lay ahead for me as head coach of the Dartmouth women's swimming team.

Coaching at Dartmouth was an incredible opportunity for me. I was determined to get the most out of whoever showed up for

11 Like the Olympics, the Goodwill Games were held every four years and attended by athletes from nations all over the world. The Goodwill Games occurred five times from 1986-2001 but were then canceled.

practice, regardless of whether they were fast or talented swimmers. I encouraged them to connect to their goals – *their* goals, not my goals for them. This meant that some students stepped away from swimming because they realized they didn't have any goals and weren't interested in college swimming. Some had focused on swimming in high school solely as a vehicle to gain entrance to an Ivy League school, and once there, they lacked enthusiasm. That was fine. I told anyone in that position, "You don't have to swim! Go be your best self." For the women that didn't want to be there, releasing them from the team was the best option because the dead weight disappeared, freeing them from the burden of training.

Overall, the Dartmouth team benefited as they focused on goals for the students who wanted to participate. Some desired social connection and only wanted to swim to be a member of a campus group. Others wanted to swim as exercise or for stress relief. Still others had a passion for swimming and wanted to race and improve their times. I felt inspired by their energy because they were swimming for themselves. They didn't have to do it for me, for their parents, or for their club coach. It was an empowering moment for the entire team. Despite the differing individual goals, I still required them to meet the training objectives, including attending morning workouts. After several weeks, the athletes who remained felt motivated to work as a team towards their personal goals.

If you're an athlete, remember to distinguish between expectations and goals. Expecting to win or perform well is more like a wish, and we don't have control over winning. Setting goals involves planning and preparation, which creates a sense of accomplishment for an athlete.

It's never too early to talk with young athletes about their goals and distinguish between realistic targets and dreams. The teenage years are an optimal time to experiment with setting short- and longer-term goals. But, if a goal is not measurable, realistic, or timely, it's a pipe dream and often unachievable. This can frustrate young people because they will most likely fail. As an athlete, if you have a plan that includes small steps, intermediate goals, and a dream at the end, it will help your focus, dedication, and effort.

For several decades, I have kept a hard copy of a *Swimming World Magazine* quotation near me. This quote has occupied my bedroom wall, my swimming locker, and now, the desk in my office. It is a simple yet profound statement: "Don't Think Small." When I cut those words out of the magazine as a teen, they inspired me to dream but also reminded me to never stop striving. In that issue of *Swimming World Magazine*, I had read about a 90-year-old woman who was still swimming, racing, and setting records. She was an inspiration to me; it meant there were no limits. If you can dream it, you can develop a plan to achieve it. It won't happen overnight, but with determination and incremental progress, success is possible.

Age 12 at the West Virginia State Championships
receiving the 11-12 age group high point award.

Age 18 after winning the 100-meter
backstroke at senior nationals.

Age 18 after winning the gold medal in the 100-meter backstroke at the 1984 international meet.

Don't think small.

My personal mantra since age eight.

CHAPTER
7

DEVELOP GRIT AND RESILIENCE

What makes one person give up and another keep striving? Why are some naturally talented athletes not the star players on their team? What separates the best from those who are good enough? The answer is grit. Grit is the ability to persevere and work towards a goal even if it's difficult. Each of us needs grit to accomplish our goals, whether in school, at work, or in life. Athletes also need it because instant success in any sport or activity is rare. As I've already stated, passion, effort, and dedication are the keys to success or achieving goals. Together, these factors develop grit.

As a swimmer growing up, I didn't know I was learning grit. By finding my passion, practicing my skills, and setting goals for myself while living in a supportive environment, I developed grit. It began when I was three years old and learned how to swim. My mom used to tell me to "kick, kick, kick." Following her instructions, I felt like a cork in the water and loved to bob and splash around. I was determined to make it to the other side of the pool, even if I got water up my nose or swallowed a gulp of chlorinated water. At a young age, I learned if I kept kicking, literally and figuratively, I could not only get to the other end of the pool but also deal with adversity. I've carried this lesson with me. Whether I have had a horrible workout, an illness or injury, heartbreak, disappointment, or failure, if I kept going, working, striving, and "kicking" towards my goal, I knew I would eventually succeed.

Swimming is an excellent sport for cultivating grit, and my mom's simple words became the basis for my efforts. Swimmers attend many many more training sessions than competitions, and they routinely establish year-long goals that require dedication and a positive mental attitude. As a young swimmer, I learned to keep kicking, taking it one stroke at a time, one practice at a time, keeping an eye on my finish line. By delaying gratification and having to wait months for the chance to achieve my goals, I developed grit.

Other sports provide the same benefit when an athlete sets goals, practices regularly, and gives great effort. If someone is passionate about their sport, they can overcome many obstacles. This resilience or toughness, which in young children might look like stubbornness or obstinance, allows a person to "bounce back" and recover from a negative experience. Disappointment is only a setback or delay in reaching one's goal. You may recall the story about me not being able to beat Julie or Kim when I was a young age-group swimmer at the YMCA. I had compared myself to them and to other swimmers. After I continued to show up at practice and give 100 percent effort, I surpassed Julie and Kim and many others because of grit. And several years later, as a ninth grader, when I quit swimming for a week, my dad's wisdom taught me more about grit. When he told me to evaluate at the end of the season, not in the middle, he reinforced the need for me to persevere, an essential component of grit. I'm so glad I listened to him. By staying focused on my goals and doing what I loved, I continued to improve in the pool.

During the summer of 1982, when I joined the Cincinnati team, I had to rely on grit just to survive the workouts. Coach Jay had a reputation for giving his swimmers "killer sets" during practice. It was the first time I had to face 10,000-meter workouts that took three hours. Swimming sets show the number of repetitions multiplied by a certain distance. When Jay had us do 100x100s, that meant we swam 100 meters, 100 times. In a 50-meter pool, that equated to swimming two lengths, 100 times. Sometimes we swam 50x200s. Whatever the set, I am certain I thought, "He must be kidding!" Sets like that were awful because they were long, tedious, and painful. During those workouts, I had to remember my goals and keep kicking to survive. I often told myself, *"I'm going to work as hard as I can today, then wipe the slate clean."* The next day or the next week of practice was something I couldn't think about. I had to focus only on the workout in front of me and do my best.

I relied on that same mindset during the high school season at the Mercersburg Academy. Each year, Coach JT gave us a diabolical swimming workout the day before we were to leave school for Thanksgiving or winter break. Before Thanksgiving, we had to swim 110x100s on 1:10. [12] Before winter break, our team had to complete 80x200s on 2:20. To withstand those grueling practices, I had to be gritty and occupy my mind for four hours. For a swimmer to survive that type of set, at a minimum, they must love swimming and have a great song stuck in their head. As I accumulated grit, it became easier to believe I would become a stronger athlete by completing those workouts.

Grit also comes into play after a failure or disappointment. When swimming officials disqualified me from the finals of a national championship race in 1983, I felt like a failure. Other athletes may feel the same when they foul out of a basketball game or fall off the balance beam during a competition. It's similar when you miss a gate and ski outside the course in a slalom race or fall onto the ice during a speed skating race. These incidents are disappointing, but they don't stop gritty athletes from continuing. The officials also disqualified me for a false start during the 100-yard freestyle finals at the 1986 NCAA championships in Fayetteville, Arkansas. After

12 In a 25-yard pool, that means swimming four lengths of the pool, or 100 yards, every one minute and ten seconds; 110 times.

cursing under my breath and storming off the pool deck, I jumped into the warm-up pool to prepare for my next race. Although I was furious with myself, the last thing I wanted to do was give up. I had to swim in other races the next day and needed to put the incident behind me and not let it ruin my meet.

Injuries are different, and thankfully, I never sustained a serious one. In 1984, while training in Cincinnati for the Olympic Trials, I experienced debilitating shoulder pain for the first time in my life. My left shoulder ached when I swam and throbbed at night when I tried to sleep. My coach suspected a rotator cuff injury. I couldn't continue training like nothing was wrong, and for a few days, I felt my dream of qualifying for the Olympics slipping away. But I refused to give up. I continued to visualize the 100-meter backstroke race and realized I could still train and prepare for the Olympic Trials, but I needed to rely on my legs. For almost six weeks, I attended every practice, but rather than swim and risk further injury, I kicked every set of every workout. Most people don't realize that swimmers generate a significant portion of their power from their legs and core. By staying positive and continuing to train, I focused on what I could do and not what I couldn't.

I mentioned Coach Richard Quick's infamous chalkboard sets at UT in an earlier chapter. Powering through those workouts required tremendous grit. Although surviving those practice sessions was a short-term goal, the training regimen was integral to the long-term objective of swimming well by the end of the season. At UT, academic classes started in August each year. Simultaneously, our team began training for the season. We did not rest or peak until a few weeks before the NCAA championship meet in March of the following year. We typically swam nine workouts each week, plus weight-training and running. The length of the tapering period would depend on whether one competed in distance events or sprints, but the entire team endured almost six months of solid training.

In my mind, I found it effective to compartmentalize each workout. I trusted my inner voice and told myself, *"I'll train as hard as I can for these two hours, then put it behind me.*" I accepted each day's results, whether good or bad, and looked ahead to the next day. Some days I felt frisky and fast, but other times I felt lead in my legs like a sinking ship. I refused to beat myself up over a bad workout because I knew I had given it my best. Even if I was slow that day, I routinely looked ahead, knowing I would have another opportunity to work hard during the next practice.

I don't think about it often, but many swimmers have a memory of their worst workout ever. One workout at UT stands out in my mind, and I relied on grit to survive the session. In May 1988, on the day I graduated from college, our coach scheduled a 4:00 a.m. practice for those of us who would attend graduation ceremonies later that day. Members of the team wanted to spend time with their family and friends that afternoon and evening, and not return to the pool for more swimming. Richard gave us the set: 12x1000s in the 50-meter pool. This was not a fun set from almost anyone's perspective because of its length and potential for loss of focus and boredom during the exercise. It took about fifteen minutes to swim 1,000 meters. After completing one repetition, we might get one minute or less of rest before starting the next 1,000 meters. Because of grit, my teammates and I made it through that brutal workout.

I also witnessed grit firsthand while coaching at Dartmouth during the 1990s. One fall, a young freshman walked into the pool area and told me she had swum in high school and wanted to swim for the Dartmouth team. She admitted her times were much slower, almost 30 seconds slower per 100 yards, than the other swimmers on the team. I found it intriguing. Why did she want to be a part of the team? Through swimming, she sought stress relief and a social connection with her teammates. I told her she was welcome to take part, but she also needed to establish training and strength goals. She agreed and joined the team.

One might assume someone in this woman's position would give up and quit. Her lack of experience and slower pace meant her teammates literally swam circles around her during practice, but this young woman showed grit. She stuck with swimming for four years, attending practices, improving her fitness and stamina, and lowering her times. When she graduated, she had dropped her time for 100 yards by over 30 seconds. Although still slower than most of her teammates, she inspired the entire group through her hard work, dedication, and grit. She believed in herself and, by being a part of the team, she made the team better. The rest of the team witnessed her unwavering commitment despite being lapped in the pool. Her teammates learned that effort mattered more than achievement, and not one team member slacked off during workouts. This young woman showed grit at every practice; she was a role model for all of us.

Years later, I discovered if I am aware of a finish line or end point, I can persist through significant obstacles. The COVID-19 pandemic, however, tested my belief when I had to close the athletic facilities at Caltech when the university sent the students home. With no idea about when we would return to normal, I had to be resilient, surrender to the uncertainty, and maintain a positive outlook. I believe those months during 2020 and 2021 were difficult for everyone, but because of grit, I could help my student-athletes get through those troubling times. By having a plan and focusing on step-by-step implementation of the plan, I reminded everyone to focus on the present instead of an unknown future. I routinely asked myself and my staff, what can we do right now to help ourselves and our students?

How do athletes develop grit? First, by finding their passion because if they don't love what they're doing, they won't show up, practice, or work hard. Second, by setting short- and long-term goals and striving to improve despite setbacks or mistakes. Third, by eliminating external pressure or stress that often accompanies peak performances, and by shifting the focus away from the outcome. Parents, coaches, and teachers can support young people by encouraging them to try new activities and by praising effort, not accomplishment. Winning doesn't matter, but effort and improvement do. Developing grit also requires time and patience for athletes to work towards longer-term goals. If a child continues to work hard and try their best, it's okay to lose the game or the race because the benefits of dedication last a lifetime. Athletes can be proud of their effort and find satisfaction in their performance or improvement. Overall, grit produces phenomenal human beings.

Age 21 racing
at the
1987 NCAA
championships
in Indianapolis.

Age 17 swimming
butterfly
at the
Mercersburg
vs. Mission Viejo
dual meet.

Pre-race focus at the 1986 world championship trials.

CHAPTER
8

MAINTAIN BALANCE

There is more to life than sports. To become a well-rounded individual, children need to explore other interests and activities. Family time, school, and creative hobbies like music or art are necessary for development; and playing with friends, reading, and enjoying nature provide balance in life. Sports don't need to occupy every night and every weekend. For many families, travel teams aren't a good choice for their child, and that's all right. Kids and parents both need downtime, and weekends without tournaments or races allow for a less stressful schedule. Parents, coaches, and teachers must encourage variety in a child's life. The key is to find balance so children may learn and grow, but still have fun.

As a young child, I swam four or five days each week for an hour or two. I attended swimming meets on the weekends once or twice each month. I had plenty of time to play with friends, help with chores around the house, and watch television or read; Winnie-the-Pooh books were my favorite. I also tagged along with my brother and his friends as they rode their bikes around the neighborhood and played in the woods. Sometimes, I helped my grandmother Faith, my mom's mom, make chocolate pudding before we played card games like War. I loved spending time with Faith, a widower whose husband, my grandfather, died a few weeks after my birth. Faith was everything I wanted to be when I grew up. She lived on her own, traveled the world, rode horses, and played golf regularly. She was dynamic and larger than life in my mind. When she died in 1996 at 93, I felt like a bright light had gone out in the world.

In Marietta, Ohio, as a child, when the weather cooperated, I sold paper cups filled with lemonade for 10 cents each on the sidewalk in front of my house. At age nine or 10, I even spent one Saturday each month "working" for my dad. He owned several parking lots in the downtown area, and I collected the rent from his tenants. Can you imagine a child walking door to door collecting a few dollars each from adults and businesses? It was the 1970s and nobody batted an eye or questioned my job. When I submitted my collection receipt to my dad, I often included a hand-written note informing him I had used a portion of the money to buy a hamburger and a Coke at Dairy Queen for lunch.

Like many kids, I also played several musical instruments, although none of them well. We had a piano at home, and I took lessons, but it didn't hold my interest. I practiced intermittently but never really learned to read music. While attending public school, I tried the French horn, trombone, and the drums. I had no talent for the horns, but I loved the drums. During music class, I banged on the cylinders and cymbals with drumsticks, eager to mimic the teacher's rhythm. When my parents refused to buy a drum kit, my fantasy of joining a rock band vanished quickly.

Although I spent time with my family and swam well during my childhood, going to camp for four weeks every summer from age 10 to 14 created my fondest memories. I loved Camp Sequoya, a camp run entirely by women for the benefit of girls, nestled in the Blue Ridge Mountains near the Virginia and Tennessee border. Camp allowed me to try new sports like water skiing, judo, archery, and horseback riding. Although I wasn't immediately good at any of these activities, I wanted to improve. It took a few summers for me to stand up and feel comfortable on water skis. I needed many lessons to conquer my fear of riding a horse. At camp, I learned to build a campfire and sail a small sunfish. Even though I never mastered sailing, every summer I aimed to sail the boat by myself. Campers performed chores like gathering kindling, washing dishes, and mucking out the horse stalls. We tidied our cabin weekly before inspection. I looked forward to roasting marshmallows around the campfire but didn't enjoy singing. To conceal my off-key pitch, I often mouthed the words or sat silently while others sang camp songs. Sunday mornings brought an hour of reflection where campers and counselors shared their thoughts or poems with the group. Listening to others brought out the creative side in me and I routinely scribbled in my journal or wrote letters to my parents.

At that age, I didn't dream about being an Olympian. I wanted to be a camp counselor so I could drive the ski boat and handle the horses. The young women, mostly college students, who operated the camp were incredible mentors and role models in my life. They were leaders and as capable as men. I also had a girl crush on the lead counselor, Nancy. I wanted her job, her energy, and her life. Besides providing balance, by attending summer camp, I gained the confidence to be myself and take risks.

While relishing my time at Camp Sequoya, I forgot about swimming. I knew the pool and practices would be there when I got home, and I never fretted about missed workouts or competitions. When I returned home after four weeks at camp, my swimming coach often penalized me for missing weeks of practice. He signed me up to swim the most brutal events at the next meet: the mile, the 400 individual medley, and the 200 butterfly. These weren't my favorite events, and he knew it, but swimming those races didn't bother me because they only lasted a few minutes. The temporary pain I experienced during those races did not compare to the lasting joy I felt being at camp. I didn't complain to my coach or to my parents about the punishment and rationalized that the next swimming meet was simply part of my training; a worthwhile trade-off for going to camp.

During the summer when I was 14 years old, my parents had planned a family vacation in Europe. For nearly four weeks immediately after school had ended, we traveled through France, Germany, Italy, and the Netherlands. I felt a world away from Appalachia when we toured ancient castles and cathedrals and sat down for dinner at 9:00 p.m. The trip brought history to life when we toured the beaches of Normandy in France and visited Anne Frank's house in Amsterdam. Hearing others speak multiple languages piqued my interest, and I studied French in high school. That summer, when we returned to Ohio, I immediately departed for Camp Sequoya and spent another four weeks away from home. My coach was furious that I had missed almost an entire summer of training, but it didn't bother me. I returned to the pool and worked hard to regain my fitness. Swimming was there for me when I was ready. Even as a teenager, I understood that swimming occupied only a part of my life; it was not my whole life. At some point in the future, I would stop swimming and continue with every other aspect of myself.

At the Mercersburg Academy as a high school junior and senior, I also found balance in my structured life. The swim team only practiced during the afternoons, leaving mornings for sleep and classes. We didn't train on Sundays, and I used that time to catch up on sleep, finish homework, and hang out with friends. My life wasn't one-dimensional, and classwork took precedence over athletics. Looking back at my teenage years, I took a lot of time away from training to enjoy life. I never saw myself as just a swimmer. I saw an individual who loved nature, adventure, traveling, and time with friends.

Even in college at the University of Texas, I carved out time for myself. My coach trusted my decisions and choices, for which I am grateful. As a teen, I had learned what I needed to do to perform my best in the pool and sometimes I needed a break from training. This wasn't unusual for swimmers or athletes, but acting on my own and doing something about it was. I understand my teammates took umbrage one weekend in the fall of 1984 during my red shirt year, when I skipped the Saturday workout and drove from Austin to Dallas for the annual Texas versus Oklahoma football game. My bold move had made some waves. Unless you were deathly ill, you didn't miss a workout. Even athletes with injuries came to practice. But I didn't leave Austin to avoid Saturday practice, no matter what my teammates thought. I went to Dallas to see friends and have a little fun. From this trip, I learned to always follow my gut and do what felt right for me, even if others didn't agree.

I did that a few years later, after completing a spectacular 1986-87 swimming season with the Longhorns. When I had finished a summer school class, even though I trained with the team in Austin, I took the rest of the summer off and didn't travel with Team USA. I had qualified for the Pan-Pacific Swimming Championships, but passed on the opportunity. [13] It would have been fun to travel to Brisbane, Australia, but I needed a break. Others may have found this odd since I was at the peak of my swimming career, but I wanted time away from the sport, a chance to rest my muscles and my brain. My boyfriend and I drove to my hometown, Marietta, Ohio, to recharge our batteries while spending time with my parents. We cooked and gardened with my mom and played golf with my dad. I showed my boyfriend around town and took him for a drive down a street called "Betsy Mitchell Lane," which extended between the Marietta YMCA and McDonald's. Even though my senior year of college lay ahead, I stayed out of the pool. I needed time away to feel excited and rested for my final year of collegiate swimming.

Years later, in 2003, I left the Laurel School without another job lined up. I used the time to reconnect with my love of nature

---

13 The Pan-Pacific Swimming Championships are a biennial competition founded by the swimming associations from Australia, Canada, Japan, and the United States, as a counterpart to the European Swimming Championships.

and enrolled in a 10-day National Outdoor Leadership Skills course. I had already worked as a collegiate swimming coach and a high school athletic director, but I wanted more leadership training. In the rugged setting of the Cascade Mountain Range in Washington, I learned practical tips on leading groups, as well as survival skills. I think it's important to continue learning, no matter your profession or job title. Knowledge is power, and as athletes and citizens, we must keep educating ourselves and others.

When I remember my childhood, I had time for school, sports, family, and friends, while getting a full night's sleep. Now, as an athletic director, I ask myself what really matters in life. I chose to direct the athletics, physical education, and recreation programs at Caltech because the job fit my philosophy of living a balanced life. Pasadena is a beautiful city near the mountains and the ocean. The community of people is supportive and caring. The weather is fantastic. I find the job challenging and fulfilling, and it initially piqued my interest because the athletic program seemed like a blank slate. The administration didn't know what to do with the program or where to start, since they had neglected athletics for so many years. How could I pass up an opportunity like that? Caltech is an NCAA Division III school and requires that undergraduate students earn physical education (P.E.) credits. The university supports my belief that it's important to challenge yourself physically and mentally. By requiring P.E. courses, the university focuses on fitness and exercise to relieve stress and bolster a healthy lifestyle.

Most adults strive for balance in their lives. They want time for work, family, sleep, and hobbies. That is a lofty goal and requires patience, but it is possible to achieve. Most parents want the same balance in their children's lives, but attending practice every night and games every weekend are not the solution. Rushing from home to practice and from school to practice while doing homework and eating meals in the car is exhausting and unhealthy. Sometimes, less is more. Letting go of one activity or reserving at least one weekend each month for family activities allows for balance. If we as parents, coaches, and teachers enjoy a variety of activities and take time to rest, we demonstrate balance for our children. And as adults, we're in charge of our kids' schedules. Parents can say "No" to extra activities or ask the child to choose a single sport or team each season. To achieve balance, we must slow down and give ourselves a break. When we do, finding balance makes our lives more enjoyable.

Age 5 selling lemonade
(me in the middle) with
neighborhood friends.

Age 7 enjoying nature with
my Grandmother Faith.

Age 27 with my
first dog Jasper,
a black lab.

Sailor's cap and campfire at Camp Sequoya.

CHAPTER
9

CULTIVATE KEY
RELATIONSHIPS

We don't live our lives in isolation. Regardless of age, activity, or goals, relationships play a significant role in our lives. We need others for love, support, and guidance. For most people, our first conscious relationship is with parents and siblings. My parents provided (and still provide) unconditional love and support. As a child, that didn't mean I could do whatever I wanted. My parents scolded me for unacceptable behavior and punished me for any misdeeds. They made me sit in an upright wooden chair in the hallway of our house when I misbehaved. It was a version of "time out." They told me to remain quiet and reflect on my behavior. My parents also guided me with their words and actions. They showed common courtesies by saying please and thank you, opening doors for people, and being punctual. By living their lives, my parents taught me how to navigate the tightrope of life between choices and consequences. I learned chores were important, and my mom and dad wouldn't tolerate a sassy mouth. Their authoritative yet loving style of parenting allowed me to take risks, make mistakes, and find fun in life. They encouraged and supported my swimming, but didn't make demands or force me to practice. They let me captain my ship.

Parents play a significant role in their children's development. A father's attitude about sports rubs off on his child. A mother's behavior towards her child's coach, teammates, and the game's referee influences the child. We are all role models, and as parents, we need to set an excellent example. Unless you are the coach or the situation is unsafe, don't instruct your child during their games or argue with an official. Applaud excellent play from all athletes, not just your child's or your child's team. Parents are cheerleaders and serve an important supporting role: to help make amateur sports fun, safe, and a positive influence in their children's lives.

I wasn't "popular" at school, and it didn't bother me because

my home life, swimming schedule, and goals kept me busy. If I wore the "wrong" brand of shirt or shoes, I didn't care. I wasn't upset about being left out of other kids' birthday parties or sleepovers.

My parents raised me to be confident and self-aware. They trusted me and I learned to trust myself. By my teens, I had little need for approval or validation from others and have no memories of wanting to blend in or conform. I knew what felt right to me and I refused to let others tell me differently.

The relationship between an athlete and their coach is also extremely important. A coach may be like a surrogate parent for some, and their words and actions have the power to build or destroy. I wanted to please my coaches, much like I wanted to please my parents.

My coaches occasionally used foul language or threw a kick board at us while we swam, but I always felt comfortable and safe.

Young athletes and parents need to keep their eyes and ears open in these relationships. If something is consistently off or seems wrong, it may be time to find a different coach, team, or sport. No championship, title, or team membership is worth sacrificing self-esteem or risking injury.

Athletes and their parents always have a choice. Other programs exist that may better fit their personality, style, schedule, or goals.

Coaching styles range from being indifferent or distracted to authoritarian and mean. The best coaches fall somewhere in the middle and bring out the best in their athletes. Good coaches don't make the game about themselves. They teach skills and encourage effort, a positive attitude, and fair play. Good coaches communicate well and lead by example. They focus on fun, learning, and improving skills. We can't expect all athletes to respond the same way to their coach. Some kids need more attention, encouragement, or guidance; others prefer to be left alone with only occasional instruction. Whatever the sport, it's important to find a good fit for your child. Find a coach who instills confidence and exudes positive energy at practice and during games.

But remember, the relationship between a coach and an athlete is a two-way street. The athlete must be engaged, communicative, and willing to work hard. Depending on the team and the sport, a coach will make decisions based on their athletes' attitudes and behaviors. Constructive or even critical feedback from a coach is often difficult to hear but is an essential part of the process. As a swimmer, I accepted feedback from my coaches and tried new techniques and training methods at their suggestion. I occasionally filtered their advice, but I was always willing to listen. In a word, I was coachable. Again, there is an important gray area between an athlete accepting everything a coach suggests versus using sound judgment about what is reasonable.

Athletes (and parents) need to be open to criticism and be willing to make changes. I routinely weighed a coach's advice and proceeded according to what felt right for me.

I swam for some amazing coaches during my youth. They were good people who communicated well, exuded positivity, and respected me as an individual. Each coach influenced me differently. At the Marietta YMCA, Coach Jim created a playful atmosphere that made swimming practice fun. For me, Jim was the ideal coach because I felt no pressure to perform, and I learned that working out could be fun. Coach Tom at the Parkersburg YMCA had a more boisterous style. He coached older kids, so his bold personality worked well with teens. Tom was as energetic as Jim, but more serious about the swim training.

At the Mercersburg Academy, Coach JT acted like a masterful psychologist and everything he said (or didn't say) got a reaction from his athletes. I remember a few workouts when I strained to make the interval and wasn't getting any rest. That means I literally stopped at the wall to take a quick breath, glance at the pace clock, and push off again. When he noticed me lagging, he said to me, "If you can't do it, move to a slower lane." Many athletes might not respond positively to that type of reverse psychology, but it worked for me, and JT knew it. I clenched my jaw and scowled, thinking to myself, *I am not moving to a slower lane. I can do this set.* Ignoring his suggestion to change lanes, I pushed myself to go faster. Other times during an intense workout, when I struggled to complete a set, JT would say, "Just give up." Although other athletes might view that as permission to slack off or take a break, I found it helped me develop mental toughness. I refused to quit, and JT's coaching not only increased my stamina but gave me confidence; I could do the work.

When I trained in Cincinnati with Coach Jay, I learned how to stay within myself during practice. Jay was often a hard-ass just to be a hard-ass. Or that's how it seemed. Other swimmers in his program would probably agree. Even though he believed swimming more distance was best for everyone, that type of training didn't always work for me. I finished the sets with the group but changed small portions to fit my level. If the set required breath control, for example, breathing every seventh stroke, I changed it to every five to stay in control. If the set required sprinting every third length, I sped up but didn't sprint. I appreciated the coaches who explained why we needed to swim those lengthy sets and put in base yardage, but Jay wasn't fond of explanations. He expected respect and compliance, especially from his elite team members. I quickly learned to look inward, encourage myself, and handle the work, but not beat myself up if I wasn't as fast as my teammates.

When I chose UNC for college, I thought it was my dream school. I soon discovered it was not the best choice for me because I didn't connect with the swimming coach. I tried to talk with him about my life and training because, in my experience, talking to adults was the best way to solve a problem. He didn't listen to me, and our communication faltered. In addition, UNC ignored my academic interests. I wanted to study education, but the university funneled me into business courses because an academic advisor felt I was better suited for business. Life became doubly difficult. I didn't like the classes, and I didn't look forward to the workouts. Swimming was no longer fun. After struggling through most of my freshman year, I looked inward and left UNC.

I transferred to the University of Texas at Austin in order to swim for coach Richard Quick and the Longhorns team. It was one of the best decisions I have ever made, and I enjoyed the peak of my swimming career in Austin. As a member of the Texas team, I swam my best races and fastest times, and I had the privilege of training with some of the finest swimmers in the nation. My backstroke lane partners, Debbie Risen (national champion) and Tori Trees (1984 Olympian), challenged me during every workout. Racing against the best every day in practice made me a faster swimmer. It was the ultimate collaboration of athletes pushing each other and improving together. I never felt like I had to beat my teammates during workouts, but I thrived on working hard and striving to be the best. At Texas, I learned the importance of having a team in individual endeavors. We supported each other at practice, encouraging each other to finish a hard set. During every competition, we cheered for each other. We gave each other a shoulder to cry on when someone missed making an NCAA qualifying time standard. If a teammate scored poorly on a test, we raised her spirits. We suffered together in the pool as we kicked sets while wearing tennis shoes or sprinted while wearing swimming suits with pockets to create drag. It was a unique feeling for me to let go of my individual aspirations and focus on team achievement.

Richard Quick was also an incredible coach for me. As the University of Texas women's head swimming coach, he demanded that I be good. He often told me, "Help yourself be better." I incorporated this phrase into my training and asked myself, *Was I doing everything I could to improve?* If not, I could only blame myself for the results. A coach leads and guides but cannot do the work for the athlete. I controlled my training, action, and effort. Only I could make myself better. When Richard pushed me to work harder by swimming in a faster lane or attempting faster intervals, sometimes I pushed back. I didn't think I could handle the work, but his confidence in my ability made me want to try. At those times, I left my comfort zone and challenged myself because my coach thought I could do more. He told me to "find a way to go faster," because he believed in me. When Richard demanded, I often questioned his demands. For instance, during the summer of 1987, he insisted I train through July and into August and compete for Team USA. I said "No" because I knew I needed a break from training. I didn't resent Richard for making demands when I couldn't give him what he wanted, and he didn't hold a grudge against me for asserting myself and putting my needs first. We respected each other's opinions, even when they differed. We admired each other's talent and drive. I have no doubts swimming for Richard and the Longhorns team allowed me to become the best athlete and person I could be.

The University of Texas women won four NCAA swimming and diving national championship titles during my time in Austin, and I had the privilege of competing for the Longhorns team during three of those seasons (1988, 1987, and 1988). Besides living and training together, we also enjoyed life in Austin, eating gingerbread pancakes at Kerbey Lane Café, munching pizza at Conan's, and snacking on chips and queso at Chuy's. We walked the Drag

(Guadalupe Street next to campus) and shopped at the Cadeau or Bevo's Bookstore. On lazy Sunday afternoons, we often sun-bathed on the roof of Kinsolving dormitory or played pool and darts at Showdown. Weekend nights might include a football game, dancing at the Boathouse near Sixth Street, or hanging out with members of the men's swimming team at a party. Our teams were close knit and to me, it felt like an extended family. Some of my teammates remain my dearest friends. We share a common history and remain close despite elapsed time and physical distance. These women are also the reason I excelled in the pool. It's no surprise that my favorite part of my swimming career was my collegiate experience.

Dr. Donna Lopiano, the women's athletic director at Texas, also influenced my life. When I first arrived in Austin, she spoke to the new female athletes during orientation. She told us we have the world at our beck and call. The university would do everything they could to help us. All we had to do was work hard, represent ourselves and the university well, and be great teammates. Hearing those words was like a dream and I thought, if I could be an inspiration like that and provide similar opportunities for others, that would be amazing.

That's why I became a coach. Competing in sports affected my life in a myriad of ways for the better and I wanted to share my knowledge and skills with others. Dr. Lopiano's leadership and involvement as a supportive athletic director planted the seed in my brain that I wanted to pursue a career in sports administration. With the university's help, I created my major in education and sports administration. And now, as an administrator, I believe hiring the best coaches and staff is the most important aspect of my job. Student-athletes won't spend their precious time playing sports if they're not finding something of value in those relationships.

One benefit to competing during the 1980s was the lack of social media. Amateur athletes didn't have a "relationship" with the public. Unlike today, where instant messages and posts abound, there was little external pressure to perform because very few people followed sports like swimming. If the public had any expectations for the University of Texas team, we remained unaware and could enjoy our anonymity. Nobody except our coach seemed to care if we performed poorly at a meet. The newspaper may have printed a few articles about the team, particularly during the NCAA championships, but other articles were rare. Overall, the public didn't comment on swimming races or criticize swimmers for poor performance. If an athlete felt pressure, it was most likely self-inflicted. Each of us can be our own toughest critic.

There was one moment, however, when I felt the heat of public scrutiny. After I had broken the world record in the 200-meter backstroke, a reporter asked me during an interview, "How could you go that fast without juicing?" The question shocked me; it felt like an accusation that I had somehow cheated. I clarified I had never used steroids or performance-enhancing drugs and was certain the reporter wouldn't ask the same question to the male swimmers who had broken world records at the same meet. I also replied that I swam that fast because of my intense training program and years of dedication to the sport.

People have also asked, "When you went out to a restaurant in Austin, didn't people point fingers and whisper, 'there's an Olympian in the room?'" I had to laugh because no one in Austin knew who I or any of the other swimming Olympians were. [14] In the 1980s, only football players had to handle that type of fame and notoriety. We swimmers lived our lives quietly, just the way I liked it.

Children depend on their parents for love and guidance. Kids want to please their parents and do what they're told. Parents must ensure that sports remain a safe, fun, and stress-free activity for children. During adolescence, classmates, teachers, and coaches

---

14 While I attended The University of Texas at Austin (1984-1988) and swam with the Longhorns team (1985-1988), the following other swimmers were also Longhorns and members of either the 1984 or 1988 United States Olympic Swimming Team: Beth Barr, Tiffany Cohen, Leigh Ann Fetter, Andrea Hayes, Whitney Hedgepeth, Susan Johnson, Tracey McFarlane, Kim Rhodenbaugh, Carrie Steinseifer, Jill Sterkel, and Tori Trees.

have more influence on kids' lives, but parents are still important. They create the framework for a healthy, balanced life. And parents provide the behind-the-scenes support of driving to practice, cooking meals, and laundering clothes. Like an athlete, a parent's effort and behavior matter. By staying positive and encouraging, but not overburdening their children, parents have the power to keep sports fun and stress-free.

The relationship between a coach and an athlete requires trust and positivity. Both parents and athletes need to be aware of potential problems and make a change if troubles arise. For young adults, a coach must instill confidence and show respect. If an athlete feels marginalized or invisible, figure out why and then revise the plan. Find a different coach, team, or activity. Finally, one of the best parts of competing in amateur sports is the friendships you make. Find like-minded people who nurture growth and encourage improvement. These qualities are the essence of a positive relationship, and these friendships can last a lifetime.

Age 16 with Mom, brother Peter, and Dad.

Age 17 when I graduated high school from the Mercersburg Academy. From left to right: My mom Diane, me, Grandma Martha, my Grandmother Faith, and my Aunt Nannette.

Age 3 with my beautiful mom, Diane.

Richard Quick, The University of Texas at Austin women's coach.

John Trembley, head coach at the Mercersburg Academy.

Jay Fitzgerald, Cincinnati Pepsi Marlins coach.

Parkersburg YMCA coach, Tom Phillips.

My first coach, Jim Everett, at the Marietta YMCA.

CHAPTER 10

CONFIDENCE IS EARNED

If you don't believe in yourself, nobody's going to believe in you. My first YMCA coach often repeated those words to our swimming team. Although it's nice to hear someone else say they believe in you, others can't give you confidence. To be self-confident, you must hear the positive voice inside your own head. You must believe you can do it. It's never too early to encourage a positive internal voice in young athletes. People may tell you, "You can't," or "You're not good enough," but if you believe in yourself and concentrate on your goals, you can combat the negativity. To live your life and achieve your goals, you need a positive voice inside your head.

Confidence is messy and requires a bit of selfishness. You must focus on yourself because nobody is going to build you up unless you act on your own behalf first. I consider this a good selfish, and one that allows you to take care of your interests, but not at the expense of others. We must each learn to care for ourselves. When you act confidently, it doesn't mean you have zero doubts or concerns. Confidence grows slowly from the inside as you work towards a goal and show improvement. Sometimes people equate confidence with arrogance, but they're totally different. A confident person believes on the inside they can do it and takes active steps to achieve their goals. There is no need to announce their progress or share their success with others. An arrogant person boasts about their goals and achievements to make themselves appear confident, even if they don't truly believe in themselves.

I keep a quote from Mel Robbins on my refrigerator that reads, "Proceed as if success is inevitable." To me, this means I believe in my abilities and my decisions, and with some positive self-talk, I will achieve or make progress towards my goals. There have been several crucial times in my life when I believed in myself and made tough decisions. The first was when I left home during high school and enrolled at the Mercersburg Academy. Although I discussed several boarding school options with my parents, they allowed me to choose the school that seemed best for me. And I needed confidence to move away from home, attend a school where I didn't know anyone, and continue swimming at a high level.

I relied on my self-confidence during my freshman year of college when I left UNC without an actual plan. The day after the NCAA swimming championships ended, I dropped out of school, loaded up my car, and drove home to Ohio. I called my mom before I left and told her I was coming home. She was delighted because she thought I would be home for spring break. I didn't tell her the entire story until later. I had given up a full scholarship and had no definite plans about what to do next. Most people don't leap without a net, but I was confident I would figure it out. My parents understood I didn't want to stay at UNC, and training for the 1984 Olympic Trials was my primary goal. My parents may have questioned my choice, but they didn't dissuade me or stop me. They allowed me to sink or swim, fail or succeed with my decision.

My parents challenged my reasoning for choosing the University of Texas at Austin, a school that already had two great backstroke swimmers and no scholarship money for me. I dug in my heels and insisted it would work out. Today, the transfer portal makes it easier for student-athletes to change schools, but I know I was extremely lucky for the opportunity to transfer. I am also grateful to my parents for supporting my decision and for helping me financially. Texas was the best place for me to achieve my potential; I felt it in my gut. I remembered watching the Longhorns team at the 1984 NCAA championship meet where they won their first national title. The women were a sorority in the best sense. They smiled and cheered for each other. They hugged and cried with each other. I respected their coach and felt a familial bond with the athletes. Most of the swimmers came from the Midwest like me, and I related to their history and upbringing.

During my collegiate years, particularly from 1986 to 1988, I dominated in the pool. Without confidence in my ability and belief in my goals, I never would have been able to achieve such success.

In 1988, after completing a stellar collegiate swimming career and graduating with a Bachelor of Science degree in education, the Seoul Olympics loomed. As my teammates and other swimmers throughout the country prepared for the Olympic Trials, I told Richard Quick, my coach, that I wouldn't be swimming the 200-meter backstroke. This shocked him because I held the world record in the event and at the time was the fastest woman in the United States. During a meeting, he told me I had to swim the event. Shaking my head, I told him no. I felt some pressure as the world record holder, but in my heart, I knew my best swim was behind me. I had zero goals in the 200 backstroke. Richard insisted I swim the event and told me he would enter me in the race, anyway. I shrugged and said, "Do what you want. I won't show up for the race." He was incredulous, but I refused to let anyone force me to do something I didn't want to do. At the 1988 Olympic Trials, I did not swim the 200 backstroke and have no regrets. Although others may have seen my choice as giving up, I saw it as taking charge of my life. My decision benefited another athlete who really wanted to swim the event.

I needed confidence to leave swimming after graduation and earn my first paycheck. I worked at the Mercersburg Academy as Alumni Secretary and assistant swimming coach. As I prepared for the job, my dad shared his wisdom with me once again: "Work harder than you think you can." He told me to be a team player, do any task required even if it wasn't part of my job description, and not take advantage of my employer. "Don't betray their trust," he said. "Even small things like envelopes, stamps, and paper belong to the school. Taking them is stealing." I heeded his advice and have done my best to remain trustworthy in everything I do.

After working for a year at the Mercersburg Academy, I returned to school in Austin with a desire to earn a master's degree in education. Dr. Donna Lopiano acted as my mentor and guided me through the program. On some level, she may have believed I wanted to follow a rigid path to sports administration and join the staff at Texas as an assistant, but I rarely follow a direct path. I knew what I didn't want to be. I didn't want to live in the infamy of an external reward. Some of my Olympic teammates slept with their medals on. They struggled to move on as if they felt they had lived the greatest part of their lives before they were 25 years old. I didn't want to rest on my laurels and take a job only because I was an Olympian. Although that status opens doors, I wanted to prove to myself I was smart and had skills to share with others.

At the end of my master's in education program, I again sought advice from Donna Lopiano. I told her I planned to assume the women's head coaching job at Dartmouth College. She told me I was "aiming too low." I believe she thought a coaching job would stunt my career or restrict me from becoming an administrator. She may have had the misconception that because I was an Olympian, I only wanted to work with the best athletes. I never asked Donna to explain her response, but I disagreed. The Dartmouth women's swimming program was in shambles. The team hadn't won a meet in decades, and everyone knew they were underperforming. They needed a leader. It was the perfect job for me since the only way to go was up and I was ready for the challenge.

I relied on my confidence to coach at Dartmouth. I had never been a head coach, but I had experience training and being coached. Without an assistant or team manager, I tackled the position alone. To prepare, I read books on the subject and talked with other coaches. My goal was to combine many of the best traits of my former coaches with an understanding of the task before me. I had to adapt training to a group of athletes with varied levels of fitness, skill, and experience. I learned to make a plan and implement the plan. If things didn't go well, I simply changed the plan.

My experience as a collegiate coach was one of the most rewarding in my life, and if I had succumbed to another's expectations, I would have missed the opportunity. Regardless of their win-loss record, the Dartmouth women challenged themselves to perform their best. As their coach, I didn't need to win a conference championship to be thrilled with their effort and amazed by their growth. Most importantly, I realized I didn't need to care about what anyone else thought or expected of me. It was my life, and I was determined to live it based on my own values and interests.

After earning my master's degree, I decided not to pursue a Ph.D. because I didn't want to teach. My aspiration was to become a practitioner. I didn't want to talk about sports administration; I wanted to be an administrator. Athletically, I had all the degrees you needed: Olympic medals, world record, world champion, American records, national champion, and NCAA champion; but opportunities didn't come my way because I was a nontraditional candidate. My mentor, Donna Lopiano, was angry with me. She may have even said, "I told you so." The business side of collegiate sports was booming in the mid-1990s and I believe she expected me to be a ticket manager at a Division I university. At those schools, sports had become a commercial entity, a corporate money-making endeavor. That didn't resonate with me. I didn't want to be a marketer. I wanted to directly impact kids' lives. After coaching, I looked for high school jobs to enter the world of educational athletics. When I told Donna about the

Laurel School position, she said, "If you go to the high school ranks, you'll never make it out. You'll never make it from high school to college." My stubbornness reared its head again, and I immediately thought, *Don't tell me I'm never going to make it*. To me, it was a challenge to get where I wanted to go, but by following my path.

When I took my first job as an athletic director at the Laurel School, I relied on my confidence to handle the position. I had studied sports administration and had a vision for changing the culture of the athletic program. I also had a plan, but this time, I needed approval from the administration. If my plan was too grandiose, I had to scale it back or change it. I knew what I wanted to do but didn't have experience with how to get it done. During the previous years, to bolster my knowledge, I had taken education, business, and law classes at Harvard University. While in Cleveland, I took business and management courses at Case Western Reserve. During the 1990s, most athletic directors came out of law school or business school because they wanted to work in the marketing, facilities, and money side of collegiate sports. The other option was working on the student, coaching, and educational development side of sports. The latter piqued my interest. I didn't want to coach forever, but I needed to understand coaching if I was going to hire them, develop them, and lead them.

For about a year, I also worked as an independent consultant, and this reaffirmed I could take care of myself and work on my own. I believed in my abilities and proved it by earning money through my business. It was a creative time for me because I didn't have to align my schedule with a school year or academic calendar. I was nervous at first to rely solely on my knowledge and effort, but people were eager to hear my perspective. The skills I developed during that time solidified my thoughts on educational athletics – that sports are a safe laboratory for athletes to challenge themselves while surrounded by adults who care about their development. While speaking with students, teachers, and administrators, I learned to market those thoughts. I spoke at high schools and at the Boys and

Girls Club, with a goal to provide a different perspective. Success didn't hinge on winning. Rather, steady improvement, achieving goals, and developing self-confidence equated with success. I aimed to inspire others and generate excitement within a school or program.

As a consultant, I enjoyed a range of projects, from actual hands-on student service and leadership training to strategic program and peer reviews. I worked with Marietta College, a Division III school in my hometown, on a strategic program review. I knew the school well as a family friend was the men's basketball coach, and my parents had often hosted members of the team for Sunday dinner. Although Marietta College's baseball program was the main focal point for the college and attracted many talented players, the administration needed to decide whether to invest in and embrace athletics or cut back and focus entirely on academics. In part, after my analysis of the facilities, staff, and budget, Marietta College expanded athletics because sports programs benefited the community; they were a draw for students and helped stabilize enrollment. Marietta College also added women's sports like lacrosse and built an indoor track and recreation center for all students. Athletics became an integral part of their college program.

In 2006, I became the Director of Athletics and Recreation at Allegheny College in Meadville, Pennsylvania, and was the first woman to hold the position. It took confidence to transition to the collegiate environment, and I relied on my knowledge and experience to perform the job. Plenty of people believed a woman couldn't be a college athletic director because women didn't play football. I countered that argument with an observation that most athletic directors hadn't played all the sports in their programs, but they still administered to the needs of those athletes. I also revealed I had some football experience. In 2006, I attended the Michigan Football Women's Academy in Ann Arbor at the University of Michigan to get an inside look at the sport. We learned in the classroom and on the field. On our last day, we played a scrimmage dressed in full pads and helmets. While on defense as a linebacker, I intercepted a pass and ran it back the other way. Had we been playing the full field, I would have scored a touchdown in the Big House.

Athletes need to believe in themselves when they train and compete, and everyone needs confidence to handle their job or career. When you believe in yourself, that confidence spills over into every aspect of your life.

While living in Ohio and working at the Laurel School, I realized I was gay. I don't know if I was ever in the closet because I had liked boys and found some men attractive, but when I lived in Cleveland, I started dating a woman. I had had this vague notion that I found women attractive, but until I was 30, I had only dated men. During this period of personal discovery, I relied on my confidence and firm sense of self to tell my parents and my brother. My brother took the news in stride, but the revelation shocked my mom and dad. My parents' key question was, "How could we not have known this?" I told them they couldn't have known until I knew, and I was still figuring it out. I was worried about their reaction to the news, given my upbringing in rural Ohio. Throughout my youth, I don't recall knowing anyone who was gay.

When I moved away from Ohio with my partner, I never felt the need to make a statement to others about who I was. When I was 13 and wanted to go to the ninth-grade dance with John, I hadn't stood on a soapbox and declared, "I like this boy. I'm going to the dance with him, so I must be heterosexual." I never had a moment like that. For me, it wasn't fear of revealing my true self, I simply didn't need to label it. I've said this to others, and they think I'm out of touch with myself, but I have nothing to fear. This is who I am, and I prefer to spend my time with women. It just took me a while to figure that out. I feel comfortable with myself, and that helps me feel comfortable with others, no matter their gender or sexual orientation. If someone is uncomfortable with me, I can't do much to help them.

Today, I love my job at Caltech as the Director of Athletics, Physical Education, and Recreation. Although during the decades prior to my arrival, the school had neglected its sports, P.E. and recreation programs, the students and administration wanted improvement. Based on the university's history, I knew it was a priority to expand student focus and develop the whole person through sports and physical activity. Many faculty members and staff also desired better facilities and more opportunities for recreation and fitness. I seized the opportunity because it was the epitome of the NCAA Division III educational athletics model.

I am confident in my abilities working as a collegiate athletic director. The job requires leadership, people management, and attention to detail. I use diverse skills for planning, budgeting, and marketing, but the students are the real focus of my job. I work every day to promote student safety, integrity, and education. I don't think I know everything, but I believe I can ask the right questions, apply my model, and lead the department. But when I arrived at Caltech in 2011, I felt like an imposter. My broad shoulders and chlorinated skin were no match for the genius and ingenuity of the faculty and students at America's premier science and research university. Several faculty members refused to acknowledge my credentials in sports, and not everyone wanted to improve the athletic programs. I reminded myself daily of why they had hired me; not to teach physics or research quarks, but to reinvigorate their athletic programs.

You need confidence to try a new activity, learn new skills, or start a new job. Sports taught me confidence. From an early age, each of us needs to practice a positive internal dialogue and tell ourselves we can do it. Although it's helpful to hear praise from others, it's dangerous to rely on that or depend on outside reassurance. Whether you are young, old, or somewhere in between, practice your own positive self-talk. Use your confidence to follow your own path and ignore the naysayers. This doesn't mean you avoid listening to others or seeking advice. It means you believe in what you're doing and keep moving forward. If you make a plan, work hard, and believe in yourself, you have the confidence to reach your goals.

Practice positive self-talk with your children. Kids need to hear that voice inside their own heads when they move to a different school or play on a new sports team. Adolescents need to hear that voice when they're tempted by classmates to ditch school, drink alcohol, or use drugs. Adults need to believe in themselves when they take a new job or become parents. I also encourage you to listen to your gut. We often know when something is not right. If you listen to yourself first, and consult with others whom you trust, you can be confident in your decisions.

Finally, I urge you to simplify. When we disconnect from social media and stop caring about comments from strangers, we focus on ourselves and our children. We learn what's important in life, what matters to us, and we believe in ourselves. Only then do we truly take charge of our lives and become the best version of ourselves.

Age 15 with my dad at Mercersburg Parents' weekend.

Age 20 after the World Championships.

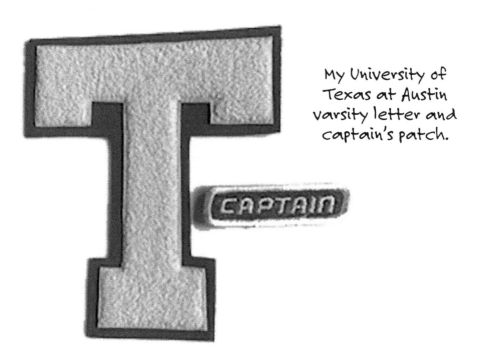

My University of Texas at Austin varsity letter and captain's patch.

Feeling confident and ready to race.

CHAPTER
11

IF YOU MESS UP,
DON'T GIVE UP

A single mistake or one poor decision can cost you the game, the race, or the championship. As disappointing as it is to lose, we know it's just a moment in time. Everyone makes mistakes and sometimes we fail, but we forgive ourselves and move forward. Athletes can do that if they find their sport fun, enjoy training, and feel motivated to work towards a goal. When the focus stays on incremental improvement instead of on the outcome, the stakes are lower and there is less pressure to perform. You can slip up and still succeed by using grit to fight through failure and disappointment. If you mess up, don't give up. Learn from your mistakes and look ahead to the next game, race, or competition.

During the summer of 1983, at the U.S. Senior National Swimming Championships in Fresno, California, the meet officials disqualified me from the 100-meter backstroke finals. Disqualifications in swimming are uncommon, but United States Swimming had recently implemented a "no false start" rule at meets. As the name dictates, if an athlete false starts, meaning they move forward or leave the starting block before the starting pistol is fired, the swimmer is disqualified. When I lifted myself out of the pool, I was spitting mad, but made my way across the pool deck to see my coach. I couldn't believe what had happened; it wasn't like me. I stood next to Coach Jay, my arms crossed over my chest, a frown fixed on my face. He seemed a bit bewildered, unsure about whether to file a protest or let it lie, but he told me, "You didn't false start. You were not the one who moved first." Although still hot at that moment, I nodded, shrugged my shoulders, and walked away. I had performed well in the preliminaries of the event, and found some satisfaction knowing I would've raced hard that evening.

The situation has stuck with me because I understand the importance of accepting the rules and the calls made by officials. In that instance, maybe they got it right or maybe they got it wrong, but the championship heat of women swam without me and there wasn't anything I could do except prepare for my next race. Although I had made a costly error, my life didn't end, and I didn't dwell on it for long. This disqualification had meant I missed qualifying for the Pan-American Games in Caracas, Venezuela, but I quickly changed my focus. [15] It was the summer after I had graduated from high school and the excitement of college lay ahead. When I returned home after that swimming meet, I enjoyed the last weeks of summer with no training. Instead, I played with my dog, gardened with my mom, and shopped for college dorm gear.

But what happens if you screw up outside the pool, court, or off the field? I have made several mistakes during my life, and the best I could hope for was a second chance, an opportunity to redeem myself, learn from my blunder, and be better. When I was a junior in high school at the Mercersburg Academy, I got caught drinking alcohol in the dorm during the spring semester. I knew it was wrong, but like most teenagers, sometimes you test the boundaries

15 The Pan-American Games are a multi-sport event held every four years in the Americas, featuring summer sports for competitors from North, Central, and South America. The inaugural Pan-Am Games were held in 1951.

and experiment by breaking the rules. It was my first experience with alcohol, and I foolishly thought I wouldn't get caught. The administration notified my parents of the infraction. My mom and dad were angry with me for my mistake because I had jeopardized my education and disappointed the school. I also had to meet with the Dean and Head of School and attend a disciplinary hearing. Mercersburg could have expelled me for the violation, but thankfully, they gave me a second chance. I received disciplinary probation for the semester and 50 hours of "guard duty" as punishment. To complete my probation, I spent several hours walking in a circle on campus, contemplating my wrongdoing. In addition, I worked on the grounds crew pulling weeds, and in the library moving bookshelves. I felt horrible for breaking the rules and had learned my lesson. Because of that incident, I'm a big believer in second chances.

While attending college in Austin, I purchased a moped to scoot around town and campus. It seemed like a great idea because the motorbike was easier to park than a car and it used less gasoline. I enjoyed riding it until I got into an accident. Luckily, the damage was minor, mainly road rash and some bruises, but I felt awful because my teammate Tracey was riding on the back when I turned a corner too fast and slid out. We ended up sprawled on the pavement as the campus police arrived to assist us. Her injuries were worse than mine, but neither of us sustained a head wound, serious cuts, or broken bones. Our coach was angry but relieved because our injuries were minor. We both took a few days off from training. My parents, after first making sure I was okay, were furious because they didn't even know I had bought the moped. After that incident, when riding the scooter, I learned to handle the corners more carefully and moderate my speed.

In August 1989, I messed up just before starting graduate school at the University of Texas. I had driven 1300 miles from my hometown in Ohio to Austin, Texas, with a U-Haul trailer hitched to my Jeep. When I approached Austin a day early, I stayed overnight in an inexpensive highway motel; I planned to move into an apartment the next day. My dad met me that evening because he wanted to review the lease agreement for me and help unload the trailer. When we awoke the next morning, my car remained in the parking lot, but the U-Haul had disappeared. During the night, someone had unhooked and stolen the trailer loaded with my furniture, clothing, housewares, and stereo. I had neglected to lock the trailer to my car and failed to back it into a parking space for additional protection. My dad and I were speechless. I felt angry, sad, disappointed, and frustrated all at once. With only the clothes on my back and a few items in my car, I learned that stuff is stuff and most of it can be replaced. Several days later, the Austin police located the empty U-Haul near a field outside of town. Weeks later, the police found my University of Texas national championship ring at a local pawn shop. The ring was the only item I ever recovered.

I have also made mistakes in my personal life. By failing to listen to my internal voice, I made a huge mistake when I was 27 years old: I got married. Mark was a great guy, and I loved him, but I succumbed to societal pressure about what women were supposed to do at that age. Marriage seemed like a logical step, even though my inner voice had told me, *you're not ready.* Ignoring my gut, I convinced myself I wanted to get married and went ahead with the ceremony. Two years later, Mark and I divorced. I felt devastated and confused. I had no problem paying attention to my gut while swimming or at work. In those situations, I relied on myself and my internal voice, but in personal relationships, it took two. When my partner's words and behavior didn't match, I lost confidence in myself. It took several years of soul-searching to discover what I needed from a personal relationship.

Working as an athletic director, I have witnessed plenty of slipups and mistakes by student-athletes. For me, they are all educational moments and second chances are necessary. Kids frequently break team rules; they're late, skip practice, or have failing grades. These situations are an opportunity to talk with the student about their lives and find out what's going on. Do they need a ride to practice? Do they need a tutor? Are they getting adequate sleep and nutrition? Is there a personal or family problem? Depending on the student's response, coaches and administrators can either step in and help or cut the athlete loose. Either way, it's a learning experience for the student. Often, they must do some soul-searching and decide if they really want to play sports.

And I still mess up sometimes. On my 50th birthday, I had a goal to perform 50 pushups in five minutes to show myself that I remained strong and physically fit. I had spent several months training and working up to that goal because I knew at age 50, my life was probably half over. Around the same time, a long-term relationship had failed, and I was approaching menopause. I had spent many years thinking about the health of others and wanted to focus on myself again and have a definitive goal. I trained at a high-intensity strength gym to regain some of the self-discipline and motivation I had lost over the years. No surprise, I sustained a shoulder injury performing 50 pushups. An MRI revealed several tiny tears of my rotator cuff and I had to rest and limit my activity for almost a year until the tissue healed. But to me, it was worth it! I achieved my goal and recaptured a smidge of my youth. I also proved to myself I was strong mentally and physically.

Whatever your dreams or aspirations, keep striving and don't give up. Despite mistakes and setbacks, if you enjoy what you're doing, keep going. Focus on your personal goals. If something feels off, or an activity is no longer satisfying, make a change. Only you know if you're reaching your goals. Don't let others define success for you. If you're happy with your life and proud of the work you do, you are successful.

GUARD/MARKS

Student ___Betsy Mitchell___   Date __3/20__

You have received _____46 + Pro_____ guard/marks for _____

___Possession & Consumption of Alcohol___.

    You must report to Ms. Kunkle or me on the front steps of Ford Hall by 8:15 a.m. this Saturday morning and every Saturday morning thereafter until this amount is walked off on the guard path. If this is in error, please contact me before Saturday. Guard is a required appointment and unless excused by Ms. Kunkle or me, you are expected to attend.

Be prompt. Saturday breakfast begins at 7:45 a.m.

                        Tim O. Rockwell
                        Dean

THE UNIVERSITY OF TEXAS AT AUSTIN
INTERCOLLEGIATE ATHLETICS FOR WOMEN
AUSTIN, TEXAS 78712

Bellmont Hall 606
(512) 471-7693

April 4, 1984

Betsy Mitchell
508 - 3rd Street
Marietta, Ohio 45740

Dear Betsy,

    Thank you for your inquiry. Please be advised that according to NCAA rules I am not permitted to talk to you about the possibility of transferring to U.T. Austin until I receive permission from your current institution to do so. Therefore, I have sent a letter to your athletics director requesting such permission. As soon as I receive a response, assuming permission is obtained, I will contact you.

    Thank you for your interest in our program.

CHAPTER
12

GET INVOLVED
AND GIVE BACK

Through years of swimming and competing in amateur sports, I've learned the importance of getting involved and giving back to the community. Many youth leagues and organizations rely on volunteers and cannot function without unpaid help. I encourage all interested parties to contribute their time and expertise to make youth sports accessible for everyone. Whether you guide your sport on a rules committee or become the coach you wish you had had, getting involved is critical for the success of amateur sports.

These days, there is also a crisis in officiating. We cannot have games, leagues, and championships without officials, but few people want to learn those skills and make those calls. The reasons are obvious. Besides pitiful pay, during the last two decades, our culture of screaming parents and ranting coaches has driven officials away. Young athletes have witnessed these tirades and don't want to step into that arena, but there will be no games without officials. We must turn back the clock and return to an era where players and parents respect referees and thank them for their work. They are human, and like players and coaches, sometimes they make mistakes. I urge parents and players to accept the call, whether right or wrong, and move on. More often than not, the "bad" calls even out for each team, and the playing field remains fair. Referees themselves are often athletes and parents. They know the sport and are doing their best to call a good game. The next time you get the urge to berate a ref, put yourself in their shoes, empathize and hold your tongue. Or better yet, get trained and become an amateur sports official.

Growing up as part of the YMCA community influenced me from an early age. My first coach loved helping people, and his exuberance shone through every day in his demeanor on the pool deck. His welcoming smile and uninhibited laughter meant he enjoyed working with kids. My later coaches also showed their commitment to amateur sports by working long hours for little pay. Their dedication instilled confidence and a strong work ethic in me. Each of my coaches positively affected my life and encouraged me to pass it on to others by becoming a coach and athletic director.

My first opportunity to lead came during high school when my coach selected me as a captain of the Mercersburg girls' swimming team. As a senior, I had high expectations for myself and the team. My coach likely chose me as a role model for the other girls because I showed dedication, followed instructions, and worked hard. I have always been the person who will stand up to my peers when I see something wrong, and I willingly voice my opinion when asked. Leading by example is my preference, showing my commitment and sportsmanship, rather than simply talking about it.

During the summer of 1985, I became an athlete representative on the Athlete's Committee at the U.S. Aquatic Sports convention. I wanted to understand the bigger picture of United States Swimming and give back to the sport I loved. The organization was mainly a legislative body, and they sought articulate, intelligent athletes willing to share their opinions. Never one to shy away from speaking my mind, I wanted to help make the sport better for everyone. Whether the issue was about the order of events at swimming meets or locations for future competitions, I gladly shared my insights at the annual convention.

Later, United States Swimming appointed me to three different committees: Athletes, Rules, and National Championship Meet Evaluation. These committees were comprised of coaches, athletes, and other interested parties, and they met annually to discuss the sport, suggest rule changes, and evaluate the national championship meet. Sharing my opinions with people who wanted to listen instilled confidence in my voice and ideas. During the 1980s, including athletes on these committees was novel. Prior to that, the U.S. Swimming organization rarely consulted athletes or asked for their opinion. I valued the opportunity to improve the sport and future championship events for fellow swimmers and coaches.

During my senior year as a captain of the University of Texas women's swimming team, I had the privilege of leading the Longhorns to a fifth consecutive NCAA championship title. Being a captain was a fantastic opportunity to get to know the younger swimmers on the team and keep myself involved at practices and during meets. I considered myself a leader and someone who tried to set a good example for my teammates, both in and out of the pool. Richard Quick, our coach, trusted me to speak candidly about practices and our schedule, and I did my best to make myself available to those swimmers looking for advice.

After my swimming career had ended, I spent time during my 20s sharing my story and giving inspirational talks at swimming clinics and meets. I enjoyed telling other young athletes about my life lessons, my successes and failures, and my desire to keep striving for excellence. My goal in sharing was never to profit from my experience or draw attention to my success, but to inspire others, and meeting those young swimmers inspired me. I remember Louisa, an eight-year-old girl in Cleveland who swam the 200 individual medley against older competitors. When I handed out medals at the meet, I talked with her about her race. I'll never forget her wide eyes and brilliant smile. This young girl's joy and enthusiasm reminded me of myself at that age.

I also spoke at dozens of community meetings and corporate workshops. Whether it was for Rotary, Kiwanis, or the Junior League, I shared what I had learned, hoping it would benefit others. In the corporate setting, I spoke to newly hired employees about work ethic and team building. Other organizations sought insight into motivation and achievement. I relished speaking about my experiences and answering people's questions. At swimming clinics like the one I attended at the YMCA in my hometown, I spoke with the kids about believing in yourself, maintaining a positive attitude, and the need to work hard but also have fun.

In 1993, I joined the Mercersburg Academy Board of Directors. After receiving a top-notch education at the school and opportunities to compete in swimming and better myself as a citizen, it was a privilege to give back to the institution that changed my life. Mercersburg also gave me my first job after I had graduated from college. Besides working on the Board, Mercersburg Academy honored me several years ago by asking me to speak at the high school graduation ceremony. I also gave the *cum laude* induction speech a few years later. After everything the school has given me, I continue to act on the Board and help steer the school toward excellence and service.

When I attended Harvard University's Graduate School of Education from 1996 to 1997, I volunteered as the strength coach for the women's crew team at Radcliffe. Although I hadn't been a competitive rower for very long, I had learned a lot about the fitness required for the sport. Working with the team in the weight room, on dry land exercises, as well as on the ergometer, a machine rowers use to simulate rowing without an actual boat, I designed a program to help the athletes improve their strength. As a volunteer assistant, I also had the privilege of coaching the junior varsity crew on the water.

When I worked as the athletic director at the Laurel School from 1997 to 2003, I craved community connection and often rented a single scull to row on the Cuyahoga River in downtown Cleveland. After meeting others who also enjoyed rowing, I volunteered with the Western Reserve Rowing Association (WRRA) and coached a youth girls' boat. Several days each week, I worked with the girls on technique and fitness. At the end of the summer, WRRA asked me to select a team of girls to compete in the Head of the Charles Regatta, a prestigious annual rowing event in Cambridge, Massachusetts. I accompanied the girls and their parents to the event and had a fantastic time. Most of the girls had never rowed outside of Cleveland and they witnessed an incredible spectacle of boats, teams, and crowds at the regatta. Thousands of fans lined the banks of the Charles River near Boston and cheered for college, national, and international teams. Because of my previous work with the Harvard crew, our team rowed out of the Radcliffe boathouse. Competing in such a premier event opened many of the girls' eyes to the possibility of collegiate rowing.

While living in Cleveland, Ohio, I also joined the local chapter of WISE, Women in Sports and Events. The group serves as a networking and mentoring community for women working in sports-related fields. I often mentored young women coaches who sought advice about becoming athletic directors. When we would meet, I listened to their history and answered their questions, sharing my perspective on an issue or problem. One of the most frequent questions dealt with how to work in collegiate sports and have a family. Although I haven't given birth to children of my own, I spent many years in a partnership and helped raise two children. During that period, I considered myself a parent and even now consider them my children. Based on my experience, it is possible to be a mother and an athletic director, but it takes patience, planning, and organization. As a mentor, I encouraged the women to reflect on their careers and determine priorities going forward. They still had to do the work, but I wanted to help them achieve their professional goals while sharing my experiences. I find the process very rewarding and I continue to be a part of WISE in Los Angeles.

I currently serve as an appointed commissioner of the City of Pasadena Parks, Recreation, and Community Services department. Appointees like me assist the city staff as we balance the interests of residents with budget constraints. We develop new parks, reconfigure existing parks and sports fields, and listen to the public's suggestions and complaints. It's rewarding to assist my local government in hearing residents' ideas as the city works to provide safe places for people to play.

In 2021, I accepted an appointment to the Division III NCAA Management Council. The Council is a group of college presidents and athletic directors who support and advise the full-time NCAA staff regarding rule changes, strategic planning, and budgeting. I'm proud to serve a four-year term in this membership organization and I truly believe the Division III model of educational athletics is the gold standard. At Division III schools, the primary focus remains on academics and student well-being while using sports to reaffirm the lessons in this book. Division III schools don't offer athletic scholarships, but many students qualify for academic assistance. Although the organization may be flawed in some ways, it's our primary vehicle to keep amateur sports alive for college-age athletes. I believe my personal and professional experience is a significant asset in this arena, and I strive to be a part of the solution. I am certain drastic changes lie ahead in collegiate athletics, particularly at the Division I level with conference realignment, and I truly hope these changes will benefit student-athletes.

People often ask me if I want to lead the athletic department at a Division I school. Although I have been a finalist for positions at Division I universities, I knew I would not be happy in that role. I don't want to be a cog in a machine. My primary goal is to have a personal influence on students' lives. I value opportunity and participation over commercialization and capitalization. My goal is to keep moving amateur sports forward for educational purposes. This may sound hypocritical since I attended and competed for two Division I schools, but through that experience, I learned I don't want to occupy a leadership position that mainly revolves around marketing and money. My joy comes from providing balanced opportunities to play, not generating revenue.

College athletics have changed. During the 1980s, except for football players, athletes maintained a simpler, almost anonymous lifestyle on campus. Before the birth of cell phones and social media, the student body and public treated most athletes like regular students. Today, many Division I athletes are celebrities. They provide their face or their voice to sell products and a certain image. I find this unfortunate because many athletes appear to be chasing NIL (name, image, likeness) dollars instead of enjoying the opportunity to play and learn. Only a slim minority of student-athletes make money from their name, image, or likeness. A few earn sizable sums, but I believe at Division I schools, scholarship athletes already have their needs (tuition, room, board, and books) met and paid for by the university. Athletes who don't receive these full benefits may seek NIL deals to offset their expenses. Although the media lures many athletes into the sponsorship frenzy with the prospect of NIL dollars, the reality is quite different. I cringe at the thought of students chasing money rather than focusing on their team and their education.

Times have also changed regarding the attitude towards non-revenue generating sports; this time for the better. During the 1980s, as athletes, we sometimes had to work and "earn" our scholarship funds by serving the university and the revenue sports. We did not get paid for our obligatory service. While I attended UNC, our women's swimming team "volunteered" as ushers at basketball games. While swimming at the University of Texas, our team cleaned up the football stadium on Sunday morning after a game. Athletes today would not tolerate this, and that's a step forward. If athletes truly want to volunteer their time, it should be with projects or organizations of their own choosing.

Throughout my working career, whether as a coach, consultant, or athletic director, my goal has always been to improve sports programs and add value. I received a bounty of opportunities and support during my years competing in amateur sports, and I want to help others as they lead sports programs and bring the joy of learning and competing to our country's youth. Whatever your interests or skills, I encourage you to get involved and give back to your community. Whether in sports, education, or the arts, join the fun, assist others, and improve the lives of our youth by volunteering. I have found great satisfaction in helping others and look forward to many more years of service to my community.

CONCLUSION:
LIFE IS MORE
THAN MEDALS

The primary aim of any contest is to win. It provides a focal point for one's efforts, but failing to win is not ruinous. It is a moment in time. Games and races have no inherent value except what each participant takes from the experience. By striving to attain a goal and testing ourselves through athletic competition, we develop character and learn valuable lessons. The opportunity to improve, make friends, and build self-confidence is the true reward. Learning grit and resilience, taking risks through trial and error, and mastering sporting behavior are skills that translate to life outside of sports. By taking a lifelong view of sports, temporary setbacks and losses strengthen us and give us resilience.

I accomplished a lot during my swimming and post-swimming careers and have benefited from all the lessons in this book. Sometimes I struggled, but I always felt supported by my parents, coaches, and teammates. They provided a positive and loving framework for my efforts. When I made mistakes, I hope I corrected my behavior and when appropriate, asked for forgiveness. I endured disappointments during my swimming career, but have no regrets, and I don't feel like I sacrificed anything in my life. Maybe I missed out on some opportunities, but I consider these choices. I followed my gut and my heart. Living in a simpler time without social media also allowed me to focus on myself and not on others. I believe people should do things they love simply because they love them. By following this ideology, I live a satisfying life. It may be idealistic or simplistic, but it works for me. I am happy and successful.

Swimming comprised a significant chapter in my life, but I always knew I would move on. I enjoyed my success, but I valued my education more than athletics. Today, television and social media offer a dangerous message that education has less value and children should compete in sports because of the prospect of money. For the vast majority of individuals, this concept is neither realistic nor sustainable. Very few athletes make the leap from amateur to professional. Instead, by taking part in recreational activities where winning has no value, we can focus on what we enjoy and how we feel. We can talk about the process of training and improving while having a good time. The true rewards involve testing yourself, striving to reach goals, and developing grit.

When done right, youth and adult sports provide so much positive energy in our lives. Staying active is critical for physical and mental health. Playing with friends promotes socialization. Win-loss records are only one metric for determining success. I believe having fun, improving skills, and building confidence are the more valuable rewards. I want the message for children, students, and amateur athletes today to focus more on these factors. We need only look to the classic baseball seventh inning stretch song, "Take Me Out to the Ball Game," for guidance: "If we don't win, it's a shame." Losing is disappointing, but it's not damaging. When we muster the courage to return to the game, we learn from our mistakes and continue developing as a person. For children, it's more important to make time to play, take a few risks, and try new activities. Whatever you decide, believe in yourself, and remember, the expectations of others aren't important.

People often ask me about my formula for success. They want to know if there is a secret sauce or magical equation. I hate to disappoint, but there isn't a formula. The ingredients that factored heavily in my achievement were genetics, genuine love of swimming, a willingness to work hard, unwavering focus on my goals, and the unconditional love and support from my parents. If any of these factors had been missing, I would not have achieved the milestones in my career.

As new swimmers set records and make their mark in the sport, older swimmers like me fade into the background. I am comfortable with that because I have other goals and aspirations in my life. But if the swimming history books mention my name, I hope to be remembered for always trying my best.

As you continue your journey in sports, I leave you with a Chinese proverb that encapsulates my personal philosophy in life:

Be not afraid of growing slowly.

Be only afraid of standing still.

TIMELINE OF MEMORABLE SPORTS MOMENTS:

1972 Joined the Marietta Marlins YMCA swimming team

1977 Joined the Parkersburg YMCA swimming team

1978 Qualified for YMCA Nationals

1981 Long Course Junior Nationals (Mission Viejo, CA) – gold medal 200-meter backstroke, silver medal 100-meter backstroke

1982 Short Course Junior Nationals (Tuscaloosa, AL) – gold medal 100-yard backstroke, gold medal 200-yard backstroke, gold medal 100-yard freestyle, gold medal 100 yard butterfly

1982 Long Course Senior Nationals (Indianapolis, IN) – silver medal 100-meter backstroke, 10th 200-meter backstroke, Rookie of the Meet

1982 USA-USSR Dual Meet (Knoxville, TN) – bronze medal 100-meter backstroke, 5th in both the 200-meter backstroke and 100-meter butterfly

1983 Short Course Senior Nationals (Indianapolis, IN) – bronze medal 100-yard backstroke, bronze medal 200-yard backstroke

1983 Long Course Senior Nationals (Fresno/Clovis, CA) – Disqualification 100-meter backstroke, 6th 200-meter backstroke

1984 U.S. International Meet (Austin, TX) – bronze medal 100-meter backstroke

1984 NCAA Division I Swimming and Diving Championships (Lincoln, NE) – bronze medal 100-yard backstroke

1984 Spring Senior Nationals (Indianapolis, IN) – gold medal 100-meter backstroke

1984 Olympic Trials (Indianapolis, IN) – winner 100-meter backstroke, qualified for the U.S. Olympic Team

1984 Olympics (Los Angeles, CA) – silver medal 100-meter backstroke, gold medal 4x100 meter medley relay

1985 Short Course Senior Nationals (Monterey Park, CA) – gold medal 100-yard backstroke, gold medal 200-yard backstroke

1985 Long Course Senior Nationals (Mission Viejo, CA) – gold medal 100-meter backstroke, silver medal 200-meter backstroke

1985 Pan Pacific Games (Tokyo, Japan) – gold medal 100-meter backstroke, bronze medal 200-meter backstroke

1985 U.S. Open meet (Austin, TX) – gold medals and American records 100-meter backstroke and 200-meter backstroke

1986 NCAA Division I Swimming and Diving Championships (Fayetteville, AR) – The University of Texas at Austin team champion; Individual champion 100-yard backstroke, 200-yard backstroke

1986 World Championships Trials (Orlando, FL) – gold medal and world record 200-meter backstroke, gold medal 100-meter backstroke, gold medal 200-meter freestyle

1986 World Championships (Madrid, Spain) – gold medal 100-meter backstroke, silver medal 200-meter backstroke

1986 Sullivan Award Finalist – Award given annually to the outstanding athlete of the year presented by the Amateur Athletic Union

1987 NCAA Division I Swimming and Diving Championships (Indianapolis, IN) – The University of Texas at Austin team champion; Individual champion 100-yard backstroke (American record), 200-yard backstroke (American record), 200-yard individual medley

1987 Honda-Broderick Cup winner in swimming; Award for top college-level female athlete

1987 Long Course Senior Nationals (Fresno/Clovis, CA) – gold medal 100-meter backstroke

1988 NCAA Division I Swimming and Diving Championships (Austin, TX) – The University of Texas at Austin team champion; Individual champion 100-yard backstroke, 200-yard backstroke

1988 Honda-Broderick Cup winner in swimming; Award for top college-level female athlete

1988 Olympic Trials (Austin, TX) – winner 100-meter backstroke, qualified for the U.S. Olympic Team

1988 Olympics (Seoul, South Korea) – silver medal 4x100 meter medley relay, 4th 100-meter backstroke

1989 Long Course Senior Nationals (The University of Southern California) – gold medal 100-meter backstroke

1990 Short Course Senior Nationals (Nashville, TN) – gold medal 100-yard backstroke

1990 Long Course Senior Nationals (Austin, TX) – gold medal 100-meter backstroke

1990 Goodwill Games (Seattle, WA) – gold medal 100-meter backstroke

1994 World Championship Qualifying in Rowing (Princeton, NJ) – gold medal women's 2000-meter double scull

1994 World Rowing Championships (Indianapolis, IN) – competitor

1998 Named to the International Swimming Hall of Fame

ACKNOWLEDGEMENTS: FAMILY, COACHES, TEAMMATES, AND COMPETITORS

None of this would have happened without my family. To my mom, a loving, structured, independent force of nature, who taught me how to swim, but more importantly, provided the best advice: "Kick, kick, kick." Before there was Dory in "Finding Nemo," who told herself to "just keep swimming," there was Diane, who told me to kick, not just in the pool, but in life, during good times and challenging ones. For my Dad who made this life possible for his family because he worked hard and showed up for his wife and children. His insistence that swimming was mine, not his, and that he would drive to practice but not wake me up to go, helped make all the difference. For Pete, my big brother, who charted his own course and never once was anything but proud and supportive. At major international meets, when the referee called for quiet, Pete was always the last, loud voice cheering, "GO BETSY!" Thank you, family! My accomplishments are yours.

To my dedicated coaches and teachers who always pushed me, supported me, and, most importantly, let me be me. I wasn't always the easiest to coach, but I was coachable! My stubbornness seemed to work out okay for me, but I know it wasn't always easy on them. Thank you, Jim, Bill, Tom, JT, Jay, Frank, Richard, and Mark. Thank you also to Barb and Liz, who introduced me to the amazing sport of rowing. I really wish I had learned it sooner in life than at 26. My teachers all along the way, especially at Mercersburg, Nancy,

Sue, Debbie, Bo, and Head of School, Walter, for always believing the best about people and for second chances. Thank you too, to the officials who worked at all the meets. Without the opportunity to race, there wouldn't be records, or order of finish, or accurate timing to mark our progress.

Thank you to all my teammates and competitors: Marlins (two different teams), Sharks, Blue Devils, Tar Heels, and Longhorns. You made it fun and gave me the opportunity to challenge myself, swim over the top of and around you, and ultimately past you. I appreciate Julie Netzel and Kim Kaufman for teaching me about goals early in life, and Sue Walsh, Linda Jezek, and Cornelia Sirch, who achieved the marks that I set my sights on. To Debbie, Tori, Jodi, and Christina, for beating me in practice every day. Your efforts allowed me to stoke the fire in my racer's gut.

And most importantly, to my friends: you are the fabric of my life. For those who have been around for a long time, words cannot express your importance to me. Ann, Betsy, Dan, and those who have come and gone, thank you for sharing the lessons and helping me grow. For those I have known for fewer years, your friendship affects my life positively every day. I am grateful to Felicia, Faith, Mark, and Brad for understanding me and accepting me as more than a swimmer. Your support helped make this book possible.

Betsy Mitchell

CO-AUTHOR'S NOTE

B etsy and I met in the fall of 1984 at the University of Texas at Austin. I was a freshman swimmer from Madison, Wisconsin, recruited to swim for the Longhorns. Although Betsy and I rarely swam in the same lane because I was a sprinter, a friendship developed between us as we trained, raced, studied, and explored Austin. During our junior year, we lived off-campus in a ratty old duplex with hordes of cockroaches and a few pesky rats. After graduation, Betsy gravitated to the northeast while I moved to Dallas, and later California. Despite our demanding jobs, family obligations, and physical distance, we never lost touch. We have often traveled together, meeting in diverse places like New Zealand, Scotland, Italy, Greece, and most recently, Thailand for hiking and cycling adventures.

When Betsy asked me to write this book with her, I was reluctant. After many months, she convinced me to work with her because her story was also partly mine. I agreed to collaborate on the manuscript because I knew it would be challenging and fun. More importantly, I agree with Betsy's message about what we learn from competing in amateur sports. These lessons apply to everyday life. In a world where kids spend more time staring at screens than playing outdoors, I believe we need to preserve amateur sports for the sake of our children's physical and mental health.

Whatever your stage in life, play and enjoy the process. Savor every moment as you learn, love, and thrive.

Ann (Drolsom) Worthington
B.A. Psychology 1988, J.D. 1991
The University of Texas, Austin

ABOUT THE AUTHORS

Betsy Mitchell is a two-time swimming Olympian, former World and American record holder, and seven-time NCAA champion. In her professional career as a collegiate coach and athletic director, she focuses on leading based on her values with a goal of maximizing opportunities for student-athletes. Betsy loves adventure travel, all recreational activities, and spending time in her garden.

Born and raised in Madison, Wisconsin, Ann Worthington is a retired lawyer and mother of two. She has published two young adult novels, and when she is not reading or writing, she enjoys traveling and spending time outdoors.

Milton Keynes UK
Ingram Content Group UK Ltd.
UKHW021049020524
442115UK00013B/432